SHIMBA
BIBLE STUDY SERIES

THE DIVINITY OF JESUS

Insights from the Book of Hebrews

Dr. Maxwell Shimba

SHIMBA
PUBLISHING

TABLE OF CONTENTS

INTRODUCTION

The book of Hebrews stands as one of the most profound and theologically rich texts in the New Testament. Unlike other epistles, Hebrews delves deeply into the divine nature of Jesus Christ, presenting Him as superior to angels, Moses, and the Levitical priesthood. It provides a comprehensive exploration of His teachings and ministry, emphasizing His role as the eternal high priest and the perfect sacrifice for humanity's sins. This introductory chapter aims to set the stage for an in-depth examination of the divinity and teachings of Jesus as depicted in Hebrews, offering lessons that resonate with contemporary believers.

The Unique Character of Hebrews

The book of Hebrews is unique in its structure and content. It lacks the usual greeting found in other New Testament letters, and its authorship remains a topic of debate. Traditionally attributed to Paul, modern scholarship suggests various possible authors, including Barnabas, Apollos, or even Priscilla. Regardless of its human author, the divine inspiration of Hebrews is evident through its profound theological insights and its cohesive presentation of Jesus Christ as the fulfillment of Old Testament prophecies and the mediator of a new covenant.

The Central Theme: The Supremacy of Christ

At the heart of Hebrews is the theme of the supremacy of Christ. The author meticulously outlines how Jesus is superior to all previous revelations and institutions of the Old Covenant. Jesus is portrayed as greater than the angels, who are God's messengers; greater than Moses, the faithful servant in God's house; and greater than the Levitical priests, who served under the old sacrificial system. This supremacy is rooted in Jesus' divine nature and His unique role in God's redemptive plan.

The Divinity of Jesus

Hebrews begins with a powerful declaration of Jesus' divinity: "The Son is the radiance of God's glory and the exact representation of His being" (Hebrews 1:3). This verse sets the tone for the entire book, emphasizing that Jesus is not merely a messenger or a prophet but the very essence of God incarnate. His divinity is further highlighted through His roles as creator, sustainer, and the one who sits at the right hand of the Majesty in heaven, signifying His authority and completion of His salvific work.

The Eternal High Priest

One of the most distinctive contributions of Hebrews to Christian theology is its depiction of Jesus as the eternal high priest in the order of Melchizedek. Unlike the Levitical priests who were subject to sin and death, Jesus' priesthood is eternal and perfect. He intercedes for humanity, offering Himself as the ultimate sacrifice, which cleanses believers from sin once and for all. This concept is crucial for understanding the new covenant established through His blood, which surpasses the old covenant based on repeated sacrifices.

The Perfect Sacrifice

Hebrews elaborates on the sacrificial system of the Old Testament, explaining how it foreshadowed the perfect and final sacrifice of Jesus. The blood of bulls and goats could not fully atone for sin, but the blood of Christ, who offered Himself unblemished to God, secured eternal redemption. This sacrificial act not only cleanses the conscience of believers but also grants them access to the Most Holy Place, symbolizing a restored relationship with God.

Jesus' Teachings and Exhortations

Beyond its doctrinal expositions, Hebrews also includes practical exhortations based on the teachings of Jesus. Believers are encouraged to hold firmly to their faith, to approach God's throne of grace with confidence, and to persevere in the face of trials. The epistle underscores the importance of faith, drawing on examples from the Old Testament heroes who lived by faith, culminating in Jesus, the pioneer and perfecter of faith.

Relevance for Contemporary Believers

The lessons from Hebrews are timeless and profoundly relevant for contemporary believers. In a world where faith can often be challenged, the epistle's emphasis on the supremacy and sufficiency of Christ provides a firm foundation. It calls believers to a deeper understanding of who Jesus is and what He has accomplished, encouraging them to live out their faith with confidence and perseverance.

Structure of This Book

This book is structured to follow the thematic flow of Hebrews, beginning with the assertion of Jesus' divinity and moving through His roles as the eternal high priest and the perfect sacrifice. Each chapter will delve into specific passages from Hebrews, providing commentary and insights that highlight the teachings and implications of Jesus' ministry. Practical applications will be drawn to help readers apply these profound truths to their own lives.

This introduction sets the stage for a detailed exploration of the divinity and teachings of Jesus Christ as presented in the book of Hebrews. By understanding the theological depth and practical exhortations of Hebrews, readers will be better equipped to grasp the significance of Jesus' work and its impact on their faith journey.

DR. MAXWELL SHIMBA

CHAPTER 01

THE SUPREMACY OF CHRIST

Divine Revelation: Jesus, the Ultimate Revelation of God

Key Verses: Hebrews 1:1-4

"In the past, God spoke to our ancestors through the prophets at many times and in various ways, but in these last days, he has spoken to us by his Son, whom he appointed heir of all things, and through whom also he made the universe. The Son is the radiance of God's glory and the exact representation of his being, sustaining all things by his powerful word. After he had provided purification for sins, he sat down at the right hand of the Majesty in heaven. So he became as much superior to the angels as the name he has inherited is superior to theirs." (Hebrews 1:1-4, NIV)

Introduction

The book of Hebrews opens with a profound declaration that sets the stage for its entire theological discourse: Jesus Christ is the ultimate revelation of God. This chapter delves into the significance of this revelation, contrasting it with previous communications through prophets, and highlighting the unique and supreme nature of Jesus as God's final word to humanity.

Historical Context of Divine Revelation

Throughout history, God communicated with humanity in various ways. These methods included direct speech, dreams, visions, angelic visitations, and through the prophets. The Old Testament is replete with instances of God speaking to individuals and nations, guiding, instructing, warning, and comforting them. This progressive revelation was part of God's redemptive plan, gradually unfolding His nature and purposes.

Prophetic Revelations

The role of the prophets was crucial in delivering God's messages. Prophets like Moses, Isaiah, Jeremiah, and

Ezekiel served as God's spokespeople. They conveyed God's laws, judgments, promises, and plans. For example:

- Moses: As the mediator of the Old Covenant, Moses received the Law directly from God on Mount Sinai (Exodus 19-20). His role was foundational in establishing Israel's identity and covenant relationship with God.

- Isaiah: Isaiah's prophecies included profound revelations about the coming Messiah and the suffering servant (Isaiah 7:14; 53:3-7), providing glimpses of God's ultimate redemptive plan.

- Jeremiah: Known as the "weeping prophet," Jeremiah's messages often centered on repentance and the impending judgment of Judah (Jeremiah 1:4-10; 29:11).

These prophets were instrumental in shaping the theological and spiritual landscape of Israel, yet their revelations were partial and anticipatory.

Jesus: The Final and Complete Revelation

Hebrews 1:1-4 emphasizes that, in contrast to the fragmented and varied revelations of the past, God has now spoken definitively and fully through His Son, Jesus Christ. This passage presents several key aspects of Jesus' supremacy as the ultimate revelation:

Heir of All Things

Jesus is described as the heir of all things (Hebrews 1:2). This title signifies His authority and ownership over all creation, aligning with Psalm 2:8, where God promises the Messiah, "Ask of me, and I will make the nations your inheritance, the ends of the earth your possession." As the heir, Jesus possesses all power and dominion, affirming His divine status.

Creator of the Universe

The passage further states that through Jesus, God made the universe (Hebrews 1:2). This echoes John 1:3, "Through him all things were made; without him nothing was made that has been made." Jesus is not only the agent of creation but also its sustainer, holding all things together by His powerful word (Colossians 1:17). His creative work underscores His preexistence and divinity, distinguishing Him from the prophets who were mere recipients of God's word.

Radiance of God's Glory

Hebrews 1:3 describes Jesus as the radiance of God's glory. The Greek word used here, "apaugasma," means "reflection" or "brightness." This term indicates that Jesus is the visible manifestation of God's presence and glory. Just as the brightness of the sun cannot be separated from the sun itself, Jesus cannot be separated from the divine glory of God.

He is the perfect and complete revelation of God's nature, in contrast to the partial glimpses given through the prophets.

Exact Representation of His Being

The phrase "exact representation of his being" (Hebrews 1:3) uses the Greek word "charaktēr," which refers to an exact imprint or engraving. This term highlights that Jesus is the exact and perfect imprint of God's essence. Colossians 1:15 echoes this truth, stating, "The Son is the image of the invisible God." In Jesus, we see the fullness of God in human form, providing a tangible and relatable revelation of God's character and will.

Sustainer of All Things

Hebrews 1:3 also affirms that Jesus sustains all things by His powerful word. This sustaining power is ongoing and dynamic, indicating that Jesus is actively involved in maintaining the order and existence of the universe. His word, the same word through which creation came into being, continues to uphold and govern all creation.

Purification for Sins

After establishing Jesus' divine nature and cosmic role, Hebrews 1:3 shifts to His redemptive work: "After he had provided purification for sins, he sat down at the right hand of the Majesty in heaven." This statement encapsulates the essence of Jesus' earthly ministry. His sacrificial death on the cross achieved the purification of sins, a task that no prophet or priest could accomplish fully. Jesus' atoning sacrifice is the climax of divine revelation, fulfilling and surpassing the Old Testament sacrificial system.

Exalted Position

Finally, Jesus' exalted position at the right hand of the Majesty in heaven signifies His supreme authority and completed work. Sitting at the right hand of God denotes a position of honor, power, and intercession (Psalm 110:1; Romans 8:34). This exaltation confirms His divinity and the acceptance of His redemptive work by the Father.

Theological Implications

The declaration of Jesus as the ultimate revelation of God carries profound theological implications:

1. Finality of Revelation: Jesus' revelation is final and complete. While God spoke through the prophets in various ways, the revelation in Jesus is full and sufficient. This finality implies that all previous revelations must be understood in light of Jesus Christ.

2. Superiority Over Prophets and Angels: Jesus' divine status and redemptive workplace Him above all prophets and angels. While they served important roles, Jesus' identity as the Son of God and His finished work on the cross surpasses all previous mediators of God's word.

3. Centrality of Christ in Faith: The supremacy of Christ as God's ultimate revelation underscores the centrality of Jesus in Christian faith and practice. Understanding and experiencing God fully comes through knowing Jesus, who perfectly reveals the Father.

Practical Applications

For contemporary believers, the understanding of Jesus as the ultimate revelation of God provides several practical applications:

1. Foundation of Faith: Believers are called to root their faith in the person and work of Jesus Christ. He is the foundation and cornerstone of Christian belief (Ephesians 2:20).

2. Christ-Centered Worship: Worship should focus on the exalted Christ, acknowledging His divine nature, redemptive work, and supreme authority. Hebrews encourages believers to approach God's throne of grace with confidence, through Jesus (Hebrews 4:16).

3. Guidance for Life: Jesus' teachings and example serve as the ultimate guide for living. His life and words provide the perfect model for faithfulness, obedience, and love.

4. Hope and Assurance: The exaltation of Jesus at the right hand of God offers hope and assurance. Believers can

trust in His ongoing intercession and His promise of eternal life (Hebrews 7:25).

Conclusion

The opening verses of Hebrews powerfully assert the supremacy of Christ as the ultimate revelation of God. This foundational truth sets the stage for the rest of the epistle, which elaborates on Jesus' divine nature, priestly ministry, and redemptive work. By recognizing Jesus as the final and complete revelation, believers are invited into a deeper understanding of God's character and a more profound relationship with Him.

In the subsequent chapters, we will continue to explore the rich theological insights of Hebrews, drawing lessons that illuminate the significance of Jesus' divinity and teachings for our lives today.

GREATER AND SUSTAINER

Christ as the Creator of the Universe and Sustainer of All Things

Key Verses: Hebrews 1:1-4

"In the past, God spoke to our ancestors through the prophets at many times and in various ways, but in these last days, he has spoken to us by his Son, whom he appointed heir of all things, and through whom also he made the universe. The Son is the radiance of God's glory and the exact representation of his being, sustaining all things by his powerful word. After he had provided purification for sins, he sat down at the right hand of the Majesty in heaven. So he became as much superior to the angels as the name he has inherited is superior to theirs." (Hebrews 1:1-4, NIV)

Introduction

The book of Hebrews presents Jesus Christ as not only the ultimate revelation of God but also as the Creator and Sustainer of the universe. This chapter delves into the theological significance of these roles, examining biblical references and employing an expository study with exhaustive Strong's Concordance to unpack the depth of these truths. Understanding Christ as the Creator and Sustainer offers profound insights into His divine nature and His ongoing involvement in the cosmos.

Christ as the Creator

Hebrews 1:2 explicitly states that through Jesus, God made the universe. This declaration aligns with other New Testament scriptures that affirm Christ's role in creation.

Biblical Affirmation of Christ as Creator

1. John 1:3: "Through him all things were made; without him nothing was made that has been made." The Greek word for "made" (ἐγένετο, egeneto) emphasizes that all

things came into being through Jesus. He is the agent of creation, bringing forth everything from nothing.

2. Colossians 1:16: "For in him all things were created: things in heaven and on earth, visible and invisible, whether thrones or powers or rulers or authorities; all things have been created through him and for him." The use of the Greek word "ἐκτίσθη" (ektisthē) for "created" signifies both the act of creation and the purpose—everything is created through and for Christ.

3. 1 Corinthians 8:6: "Yet for us there is but one God, the Father, from whom all things came and for whom we live; and there is but one Lord, Jesus Christ, through whom all things came and through whom we live." This verse highlights the collaborative work of the Father and the Son in creation, with Christ being the divine channel through whom all things exist.

Theological Significance of Christ as Creator

Christ's role as Creator underscores His divine nature and preexistence. He is not a created being but the source of all creation. This aligns with the Old Testament revelation of God as the Creator of the heavens and the earth (Genesis 1:1). By attributing creation to Jesus, Hebrews affirms His equality with God the Father and His participation in the divine essence.

Christ as the Sustainer

Hebrews 1:3 further reveals that Jesus sustains all things by His powerful word. This sustaining action is continuous and essential for the existence and order of the universe.

Biblical Affirmation of Christ as Sustainer

1. Colossians 1:17: "He is before all things, and in him all things hold together." The Greek word "συνίστημι" (synistēmi) means "to hold together" or "to cohere." This indicates that Christ is the cohesive force of the universe, maintaining its stability and order.

2. Acts 17:28: "For in him we live and move and have our being." Although this verse refers to God, it can be applied to Christ as part of the Godhead, emphasizing that our existence is sustained by His divine power.

3. Psalm 75:3: "When the earth and all its people quake, it is I who hold its pillars firm." While this Old Testament reference speaks of God, it reflects the sustaining power attributed to Christ in the New Testament.

Theological Significance of Christ as Sustainer

Christ's role as Sustainer highlights His ongoing involvement in creation. Unlike the deistic view that God created the universe and then left it to run on its own, the biblical view presented in Hebrews is that Jesus actively upholds and maintains the universe. This sustaining power is described as being executed by His "powerful word" (ῥῆμα, rhēma), indicating the authority and efficacy of His command.

Expository Study and Strong's Concordance Analysis

Hebrews 1:2 - "Through whom also he made the universe."

- Made (ἐποίησεν, epoiēsen): The verb "to make" signifies the creative act. It is the same verb used in Genesis 1:1 in the Septuagint (LXX), linking Jesus directly to the act of creation.

- Universe (αἰῶνας, aiōnas): This term can be translated as "ages" or "worlds," indicating not only the material universe but also the ages of time, affirming Jesus' role in both creating and shaping history.

Hebrews 1:3 - "Sustaining all things by his powerful word."

- Sustaining (φέροντα, pheronta): The present participle indicates continuous action, emphasizing that Jesus is constantly upholding the universe.

- Word (ῥῆμα, rhēma): This term signifies a spoken word or command, highlighting the power and authority inherent in Jesus' speech.

Practical Implications for Believers

1. Confidence in Christ's Sovereignty: Understanding Jesus as Creator and Sustainer assures believers of His supreme power and authority over all aspects of life and the universe. This confidence can foster trust and reliance on Him in all circumstances.

2. Recognition of Christ's Continuous Work: The fact that Jesus sustains all things implies that He is actively involved in the world and our lives. Believers can find comfort in knowing that Christ is not distant but intimately engaged in maintaining creation.

3. Worship and Adoration: Recognizing Jesus as Creator and Sustainer should lead to profound worship and adoration. He is worthy of all praise not only for His redemptive work but also for His ongoing role in sustaining life and creation.

4. Integration of Faith and Science: Understanding Christ as the Creator and Sustainer bridges the gap between faith and science. Believers can appreciate scientific discoveries about the universe as revelations of Christ's sustaining power and creative genius.

Conclusion

Hebrews 1:1-4 presents a majestic vision of Jesus Christ as both the Creator of the universe and the Sustainer of all things. This dual role underscores His divine nature and

His intimate involvement in the ongoing existence of creation. By exploring these truths through an expository study and analysis using Strong's Concordance, we gain a deeper appreciation for the supremacy of Christ. This understanding not only enriches our theological knowledge but also enhances our faith and worship, anchoring our lives in the One who holds all things together by His powerful word.

RADIANCE OF GOD'S GLORY

He is the Exact Representation of God's Being, Reflecting His Glory

Key Verses: Hebrews 1:1-4

"In the past, God spoke to our ancestors through the prophets at many times and in various ways, but in these last days, he has spoken to us by his Son, whom he appointed heir of all things, and through whom also he made the universe. The Son is the radiance of God's glory and the exact representation of his being, sustaining all things by his powerful word. After he had provided purification for sins, he sat down at the right hand of the Majesty in heaven. So he became as much superior to the angels as the name he has inherited is superior to theirs." (Hebrews 1:1-4, NIV)

Introduction

The book of Hebrews begins with a profound assertion that Jesus Christ is the radiance of God's glory and the exact representation of His being. This chapter explores the theological significance of this declaration, delving into biblical references and employing an expository study with the exhaustive Strong's Concordance. Understanding Jesus as the radiance of God's glory enriches our comprehension of His divine nature and His unique role in revealing God to humanity.

Radiance of God's Glory

Hebrews 1:3 describes Jesus as the "radiance of God's glory." The Greek term used here for "radiance" is "ἀπαύγασμα" (apaugasma), which means "reflection" or "brightness." This concept signifies that Jesus is the visible manifestation of God's glory, perfectly reflecting His divine essence.

Biblical Affirmation of Radiance

1. John 1:14: "The Word became flesh and made his dwelling among us. We have seen his glory, the glory of the one and only Son, who came from the Father, full of grace and truth." This verse highlights that Jesus, the incarnate Word, revealed God's glory to humanity.

2. Colossians 1:15: "The Son is the image of the invisible God, the firstborn over all creation." Here, the term

"image" (εἰκών, eikōn) underscores that Jesus is the perfect representation of the invisible God.

3. John 14:9: Jesus said, "Anyone who has seen me has seen the Father." This statement confirms that seeing Jesus is equivalent to seeing God the Father, as He reflects God's glory.

Theological Significance of Radiance

The radiance of God's glory in Jesus signifies several key theological truths:

1. Visibility of God's Glory: In the Old Testament, God's glory was often manifested in ways that were both awe-inspiring and terrifying, such as the burning bush (Exodus 3:2-6) and the Shekinah glory in the Tabernacle (Exodus 40:34-35). In Jesus, God's glory becomes approachable and visible in a person.

2. Revelation of God's Character: Jesus, as the radiance of God's glory, reveals the character and nature of God. His actions, teachings, and sacrificial love provide a clear picture of who God is.

3. Continuity with Old Testament Revelation: The concept of God's glory being reflected through Jesus aligns with Old Testament themes. For instance, Moses' face shone with God's glory after being in His presence (Exodus 34:29-

35), pointing forward to the ultimate revelation of God's glory in Christ.

Exact Representation of God's Being

Hebrews 1:3 also declares that Jesus is the exact representation of God's being. The Greek term used here is "χαρακτήρ" (charaktēr), which refers to an exact imprint or engraving, like that made by a stamp or seal. This term emphasizes that Jesus is the precise and perfect representation of God's essence.

Biblical Affirmation of Exact Representation

1. Colossians 2:9: "For in Christ all the fullness of the Deity lives in bodily form." This verse asserts that Jesus embodies the entirety of God's nature.

2. Philippians 2:6: "Who, being in very nature God, did not consider equality with God something to be used to his own advantage." The term "nature" (μορφή, morphē) indicates that Jesus possesses the very essence of God.

3. John 10:30: Jesus said, "I and the Father are one." This statement underscores the unity and identical nature of Jesus with God the Father.

Theological Significance of Exact Representation

The exact representation of God's being in Jesus carries profound theological implications:

1. Unity with the Father: Jesus shares the same divine essence as the Father, affirming the doctrine of the Trinity. This unity means that Jesus' actions and words are direct revelations of God's will and character.

2. Incarnation: The concept of Jesus being the exact representation of God's being is crucial for understanding the incarnation. God took on human flesh in Jesus, making His divine nature accessible and knowable to humanity.

3. Redemptive Revelation: Jesus' life, death, and resurrection are the ultimate expressions of God's nature and His redemptive plan for humanity. In Jesus, we see God's love, justice, mercy, and holiness fully displayed.

Expository Study and Strong's Concordance Analysis

Hebrews 1:3 - "The Son is the radiance of God's glory and the exact representation of his being."

- Radiance (ἀπαύγασμα, apaugasma): This term indicates that Jesus is the reflection or brightness of God's glory. The use of this word emphasizes that Jesus is not just a reflection but the very light of God's presence.

- Exact Representation (χαρακτήρ, charaktēr): The term "charaktēr" signifies an exact imprint, like that of a coin or seal. This word underscores the precise and perfect nature of Jesus as the visible expression of God's essence.

- Being (ὑπόστασις, hypostasis): This term refers to the underlying reality or substance. In this context, it means that Jesus is the manifestation of God's very substance and nature.

Practical Implications for Believers

1. Deepened Understanding of God: Recognizing Jesus as the radiance of God's glory and the exact representation of His being deepens our understanding of who God is. By studying Jesus' life and teachings, believers can gain a clearer picture of God's character and will.

2. Increased Faith and Trust: Knowing that Jesus perfectly reflects God's glory and essence can increase believers' faith and trust in Him. Jesus' actions and words are direct revelations from God, providing a solid foundation for faith.

3. Motivation for Worship: The realization of Jesus' divine nature and His role in revealing God's glory should lead believers to a deeper, more profound worship. Understanding His divinity inspires awe and reverence.

4. Guidance for Christian Living: As the exact representation of God, Jesus' example provides clear guidance for how believers should live. His teachings and actions serve as the ultimate model for Christian conduct.

Conclusion

Hebrews 1:1-4 presents Jesus Christ as the radiance of God's glory and the exact representation of His being. This dual role emphasizes His divine nature and His unique function in revealing God to humanity. By exploring these truths through an expository study and analysis using Strong's Concordance, we gain a deeper appreciation for the supremacy of Christ. This understanding enriches our theological knowledge and enhances our faith, guiding us in our relationship with God and our daily walk with Christ.

In the chapters that follow, we will continue to delve into the rich theological insights of Hebrews, drawing lessons that illuminate the significance of Jesus' divinity and teachings for our lives today.

PURIFICATION OF SINS

Purification of Sins: Jesus Made Purification for Sins and is Now Seated at the Right Hand of the Majesty on High

Key Verses: Hebrews 1:1-4

"In the past, God spoke to our ancestors through the prophets at many times and in various ways, but in these last days, he has spoken to us by his Son, whom he appointed heir of all things, and through whom also he made the universe. The Son is the radiance of God's glory and the exact representation of his being, sustaining all things by his powerful word. After he had provided purification for sins, he sat down at the right hand of the Majesty in heaven. So he became as much superior to the angels as the name he has inherited is superior to theirs." (Hebrews 1:1-4, NIV)

Introduction

The book of Hebrews intricately details the purification of sins accomplished by Jesus Christ, emphasizing His unique role as the final and perfect sacrifice. This chapter explores the theological depth of this concept, examining biblical references and employing an expository study with exhaustive Strong's Concordance. Understanding Jesus' work in purifying sins enriches our appreciation of His divine authority and the completeness of His salvation.

Jesus as the Perfect Sacrifice

The purification of sins is central to the message of Hebrews. The text highlights Jesus' sacrificial death as the definitive act that cleanses humanity from sin, surpassing the Old Testament sacrificial system.

Biblical Affirmation of Jesus' Sacrifice

1. Hebrews 9:12-14: "He did not enter by means of the blood of goats and calves; but he entered the Most Holy Place once for all by his own blood, thus obtaining eternal redemption. The blood of goats and bulls and the ashes of a heifer sprinkled on those who are ceremonially unclean sanctify them so that they are outwardly clean. How much

more, then, will the blood of Christ, who through the eternal Spirit offered himself unblemished to God, cleanse our consciences from acts that lead to death, so that we may serve the living God!"

- This passage contrasts the temporary and external purification of the old sacrifices with the eternal and internal purification achieved through Jesus' blood.

2. Hebrews 10:10-12: "And by that will, we have been made holy through the sacrifice of the body of Jesus Christ once for all. Day after day every priest stands and performs his religious duties; again and again he offers the same sacrifices, which can never take away sins. But when this priest had offered for all time one sacrifice for sins, he sat down at the right hand of God."

- Jesus' single sacrifice contrasts with the repetitive sacrifices of the Levitical priests, highlighting the completeness and sufficiency of His offering.

3. 1 John 1:7: "But if we walk in the light, as he is in the light, we have fellowship with one another, and the blood of Jesus, his Son, purifies us from all sin."

- This verse underscores the ongoing cleansing power of Jesus' blood for believers.

Theological Significance of Purification of Sins

Fulfillment of the Old Covenant

The purification of sins by Jesus fulfills the sacrificial requirements of the Old Covenant. The sacrifices prescribed in the Law of Moses were a foreshadowing of the ultimate sacrifice that Jesus would offer.

1. Leviticus 16:30: "Because on this day atonement will be made for you, to cleanse you. Then, before the Lord, you will be clean from all your sins."

- The Day of Atonement (Yom Kippur) involved annual sacrifices for the purification of Israel. Jesus' sacrifice fulfills and surpasses these rituals by offering a permanent solution.

2. Hebrews 9:22: "In fact, the law requires that nearly everything be cleansed with blood, and without the shedding of blood there is no forgiveness."

- This verse reiterates the necessity of bloodshed for forgiveness, which is ultimately and perfectly fulfilled in Jesus' sacrifice.

Jesus' Role as High Priest

Jesus' purification of sins is intricately linked to His role as the eternal High Priest.

1. Hebrews 4:14-16: "Therefore, since we have a great high priest who has ascended into heaven, Jesus the Son of God, let us hold firmly to the faith we profess. For we do not have a high priest who is unable to feel sympathy for our

weaknesses, but we have one who has been tempted in every way, just as we are—yet he did not sin. Let us then approach God's throne of grace with confidence, so that we may receive mercy and find grace to help us in our time of need."

- Jesus, as the sinless High Priest, is uniquely qualified to offer the perfect sacrifice and intercede on behalf of humanity.

2. Hebrews 7:27: "Unlike the other high priests, he does not need to offer sacrifices day after day, first for his own sins and then for the sins of the people. He sacrificed for their sins once for all when he offered himself."

- This highlights the finality and sufficiency of Jesus' self-sacrifice, distinguishing it from the repeated offerings of the Levitical priests.

Expository Study and Strong's Concordance Analysis

Hebrews 1:3 - "After he had provided purification for sins, he sat down at the right hand of the Majesty in heaven."

- Purification (καθαρισμὸν, katharismon): This term refers to the act of cleansing or purifying. In the context of Hebrews, it signifies the complete removal of sin's defilement through Jesus' sacrificial death.

- Strong's Concordance: G2512 – katharismós; purification, cleansing.

- Sins (ἁμαρτιῶν, hamartiōn): The term for sins denotes moral failures or offenses against God's law. Jesus' purification addresses the totality of human sin.

- Strong's Concordance: G266 – hamartía; sin, failure, missing the mark.

- Sat Down (ἐκάθισεν, ekathisen): This verb indicates a completed action and signifies Jesus' position of honor and authority after completing His work of redemption.

- Strong's Concordance: G2523 – kathízō; to sit down, to be seated.

- Majesty (Μεγαλωσύνης, Megalosynēs): This term refers to the greatness or majesty of God, emphasizing His sovereign rule and divine authority.

- Strong's Concordance: G3172 – megalōsýnē; greatness, majesty.

Hebrews 10:10 - "And by that will, we have been made holy through the sacrifice of the body of Jesus Christ once for all."

- Holy (ἡγιασμένοι, hēgiasmenoi): This term means to be sanctified or made holy. Believers are sanctified through Jesus' sacrifice.

- Strong's Concordance: G37 – hagiazō; to make holy, consecrate, sanctify.

- Sacrifice (προσφορᾶς, prosphoras): This term refers to an offering or sacrifice, specifically the body of Jesus offered for the purification of sins.

- Strong's Concordance: G4376 – prosphorá; an offering, sacrifice.

Practical Implications for Believers

1. Assurance of Forgiveness: Understanding that Jesus' sacrifice provides complete purification for sins offers believers assurance of forgiveness. They can live in the freedom of knowing their sins are fully cleansed.

2. Confidence in Salvation: Jesus' completed work of purification allows believers to approach God with confidence, knowing their salvation is secure in Christ's perfect sacrifice.

3. Motivation for Holiness: Recognizing the depth of Jesus' sacrifice motivates believers to live holy lives in response to His love and grace.

4. Encouragement in Worship: The understanding of Jesus' purification of sins and His exaltation at the right hand of God enriches worship, inspiring awe and gratitude.

Conclusion

Hebrews 1:1-4 presents Jesus Christ as the one who has made purification for sins and now sits at the right hand of the Majesty on high. This role underscores His divine authority and the completeness of His salvific work. By exploring these truths through an expository study and analysis using Strong's Concordance, we gain a deeper appreciation for the supremacy of Christ. This understanding not only enriches our theological knowledge but also enhances our faith and worship, guiding us in our relationship with God and our daily walk with Christ.

In the chapters that follow, we will continue to delve into the rich theological insights of Hebrews, drawing lessons that illuminate the significance of Jesus' divinity and teachings for our lives today.

CHAPTER 02

JESUS, FULLY HUMAN, FULLY DIVINE

Humiliation and Exaltation: Jesus, Though Divine, Became a Little Lower than the Angels to Taste Death for Everyone, Signifying His Full Identification with Humanity

Key Verses: Hebrews 2:9-18

"But we do see Jesus, who was made lower than the angels for a little while, now crowned with glory and honor because he suffered death, so that by the grace of God he might taste death for everyone. In bringing many sons and daughters to glory, it was fitting that God, for whom and through whom everything exists, should make the pioneer of their salvation perfect through what he suffered. Both the one who makes people holy and those who are made holy are of the same family. So Jesus is not ashamed to call them brothers and sisters. He says, 'I will declare your name to my brothers and sisters; in the assembly I will sing your praises.' And again, 'I will put my trust in him.' And again he says, 'Here am I, and the children God has given me.' Since the children have flesh and blood, he too shared in their humanity so that by his death he might break the power of him who holds the power of death—that is, the devil—and free those who all their lives were held in slavery by their fear of death. For surely it is not angels he helps, but Abraham's descendants. For this reason he had to be made like them, fully human in every way, in order that he might become a merciful and faithful high priest in service to God, and that he might make atonement for the sins of the people. Because he himself suffered when he was tempted, he is able to help those who are being tempted." (Hebrews 2:9-18, NIV)

Introduction

The book of Hebrews provides a profound theological exploration of Jesus' dual nature—His full humanity and divinity. This chapter delves into the concepts of Jesus' humiliation and exaltation as detailed in Hebrews 2:9-18. Understanding these aspects of Jesus' life and work is crucial for grasping the depth of His identification with humanity and the completeness of His redemptive mission.

Jesus' Humiliation

Made Lower than the Angels

Hebrews 2:9 begins by acknowledging that Jesus was made "a little lower than the angels" for a short period. This refers to His incarnation, where He took on human flesh and entered into the human condition.

1. Philippians 2:6-8: "Who, being in very nature God, did not consider equality with God something to be used to his own advantage; rather, he made himself nothing by taking the very nature of a servant, being made in human likeness. And being found in appearance as a man, he humbled himself by becoming obedient to death—even death on a cross!"

- This passage underscores the voluntary nature of Jesus' humiliation, where He emptied Himself of divine privileges to become human.

2. John 1:14: "The Word became flesh and made his dwelling among us. We have seen his glory, the glory of the one and only Son, who came from the Father, full of grace and truth."

- Jesus, the eternal Word, took on human nature and lived among us, fully identifying with the human experience.

Tasting Death for Everyone

Jesus' ultimate act of humiliation was His death on the cross. Hebrews 2:9 emphasizes that He tasted death for everyone, signifying the universal scope of His sacrificial death.

1. Romans 5:8: "But God demonstrates his own love for us in this: While we were still sinners, Christ died for us."

- This verse highlights the sacrificial nature of Jesus' death, which was done on behalf of all humanity.

2. 1 Peter 2:24: "He himself bore our sins in his body on the cross, so that we might die to sins and live for righteousness; by his wounds you have been healed."

- Jesus' death on the cross was a substitutionary atonement, bearing the sins of humanity to bring about healing and reconciliation.

Identification with Humanity

Hebrews 2:14-17 elaborates on Jesus' identification with humanity by sharing in flesh and blood.

1. Galatians 4:4-5: "But when the set time had fully come, God sent his Son, born of a woman, born under the law, to redeem those under the law, that we might receive adoption to sonship."

- Jesus was born under the law to redeem those under the law, emphasizing His full participation in the human condition.

2. 1 Timothy 2:5: "For there is one God and one mediator between God and mankind, the man Christ Jesus."

- Jesus, as fully human, serves as the mediator between God and humanity, bridging the gap caused by sin.

Jesus' Exaltation

Crowned with Glory and Honor

After His humiliation and sacrificial death, Jesus was exalted and crowned with glory and honor, as stated in Hebrews 2:9.

1. Philippians 2:9-11: "Therefore God exalted him to the highest place and gave him the name that is above every name, that at the name of Jesus every knee should bow, in heaven and on earth and under the earth, and every tongue acknowledge that Jesus Christ is Lord, to the glory of God the Father."

- This passage describes Jesus' exaltation and the universal recognition of His lordship.

2. Acts 2:33: "Exalted to the right hand of God, he has received from the Father the promised Holy Spirit and has poured out what you now see and hear."

- Jesus' exaltation to the right hand of God signifies His supreme authority and the completion of His redemptive work.

Breaking the Power of Death

Through His death and resurrection, Jesus broke the power of death and the devil, as noted in Hebrews 2:14-15.

1. 1 Corinthians 15:54-57: "When the perishable has been clothed with the imperishable, and the mortal with immortality, then the saying that is written will come true: 'Death has been swallowed up in victory.' 'Where, O death, is your victory? Where, O death, is your sting?' The sting of death is sin, and the power of sin is the law. But thanks be to God! He gives us the victory through our Lord Jesus Christ."

- Jesus' resurrection victory over death ensures believers' victory over death and eternal life.

2. Revelation 1:18: "I am the Living One; I was dead, and now look, I am alive forever and ever! And I hold the keys of death and Hades."

- Jesus' authority over death and Hades signifies His triumph over the ultimate enemies of humanity.

Expository Study and Strong's Concordance Analysis

Hebrews 2:9 - "But we do see Jesus, who was made lower than the angels for a little while, now crowned with glory and honor because he suffered death, so that by the grace of God he might taste death for everyone."

- Lower (ἠλαττωμένος, ēlattyōmenos): This term indicates being made less or inferior. Jesus' temporary lowering below the angels signifies His incarnation.

- Strong's Concordance: G1642 – elattoō; to make less or inferior.

- Crowned (ἐστεφανωμένος, estephanōmenos): This term refers to being adorned with a crown, symbolizing honor and authority.

- Strong's Concordance: G4737 – stephanoō; to crown.

- Tasted (γεύσηται, geusētai): This verb means to experience or partake in something, here referring to Jesus experiencing death.

- Strong's Concordance: G1089 – geuomai; to taste, partake of, experience.

Hebrews 2:14 - "Since the children have flesh and blood, he too shared in their humanity so that by his death he might break the power of him who holds the power of death—that is, the devil."

- Shared (μετέσχεν, meteschen): This term means to partake or share in something. Jesus shared in humanity by taking on flesh and blood.

- Strong's Concordance: G3348 – metechō; to share, partake of.

- Break (καταργήση, katargēsē): This verb means to render powerless or to nullify. Jesus' death rendered the devil's power over death ineffective.

- Strong's Concordance: G2673 – katargeō; to render idle, inactive, or ineffective.

Practical Implications for Believers

1. Empathy and Compassion: Jesus' full identification with humanity assures believers that He understands their struggles and sufferings. This provides comfort and encourages believers to approach Him with confidence.

2. Victory Over Death: Jesus' victory over death and the devil offers believers hope and assurance of eternal life. This victory empowers believers to live without the fear of death.

3. Exaltation Through Humility: Jesus' exaltation following His humility serves as a model for believers. Humility and obedience to God lead to ultimate exaltation and honor.

4. Strength in Temptation: Knowing that Jesus was tempted and suffered as humans do, believers can find strength and support in their own times of temptation and trial.

Conclusion

Hebrews 2:9-18 provides a profound insight into the humiliation and exaltation of Jesus Christ. By exploring these themes through an expository study and analysis using Strong's Concordance, we gain a deeper understanding of His full identification with humanity and His ultimate victory over death. This understanding enriches our theological knowledge and enhances our faith, guiding us in our relationship with God and our daily walk with Christ.

In the subsequent chapters, we will continue to delve into the rich theological insights of Hebrews, drawing lessons that illuminate the significance of Jesus' dual nature and teachings for our lives today.

PIONEER OF SALVATION

Through Suffering, He Became the Perfect Pioneer of Salvation

Key Verses: Hebrews 2:9-18

"But we do see Jesus, who was made lower than the angels for a little while, now crowned with glory and honor because he suffered death, so that by the grace of God he might taste death for everyone. In bringing many sons and daughters to glory, it was fitting that God, for whom and through whom everything exists, should make the pioneer of their salvation perfect through what he suffered. Both the one who makes people holy and those who are made holy are of the same family. So Jesus is not ashamed to call them brothers and sisters. He says, 'I will declare your name to my brothers and sisters; in the assembly I will sing your praises.' And again, 'I will put my trust in him.' And again he says, 'Here am I, and the children God has given me.' Since the children have flesh and blood, he too shared in their humanity so that by his death he might break the power of him who holds the power of death—that is, the devil—and free those who all their lives were held in slavery by their fear of death. For surely it is not angels he helps, but Abraham's descendants. For this reason he had to be made like them, fully human in every way, in order that he might become a merciful and faithful high priest in service to God, and that he might make atonement for the sins of the people. Because he himself suffered when he was tempted, he is able to help those who are being tempted." (Hebrews 2:9-18, NIV)

Introduction

The concept of Jesus as the "pioneer of salvation" is a profound and central theme in the book of Hebrews. This chapter explores the significance of Jesus' role as the pioneer who leads many sons and daughters to glory through His suffering and perfecting work. By examining biblical references and employing an expository study with exhaustive

Strong's Concordance, we can gain a deeper understanding of how Jesus' suffering made Him the perfect pioneer of our salvation.

Jesus as the Pioneer of Salvation

The term "pioneer" (ἀρχηγός, archēgos) in Hebrews 2:10 carries the meaning of a leader, author, or originator. It signifies one who goes ahead to open the way for others to follow. Jesus, as the pioneer of salvation, blazes the trail for humanity to follow, leading us to glory through His suffering and death.

Biblical Affirmation of Jesus as Pioneer

1. Hebrews 12:2: "Fixing our eyes on Jesus, the pioneer and perfecter of faith. For the joy set before him he endured the cross, scorning its shame, and sat down at the right hand of the throne of God."

- This verse emphasizes Jesus as both the pioneer and perfecter of faith, highlighting His role in initiating and completing the path of salvation through His endurance of the cross.

2. Acts 3:15: "You killed the author of life, but God raised him from the dead. We are witnesses of this."

- The term "author" (ἀρχηγός, archēgos) here refers to Jesus as the originator of life, underscoring His pioneering role in bringing life and salvation through His resurrection.

3. Hebrews 5:9: "And once made perfect, he became the source of eternal salvation for all who obey him."

- Jesus, made perfect through suffering, becomes the source (or pioneer) of eternal salvation, confirming His leading role in the salvation of humanity.

Theological Significance of Jesus' Suffering

Hebrews 2:10 states that it was fitting for God to make the pioneer of their salvation perfect through suffering. This indicates that Jesus' suffering was necessary to fulfill His role as the pioneer of salvation.

Perfected Through Suffering

1. Philippians 2:8: "And being found in appearance as a man, he humbled himself by becoming obedient to death— even death on a cross!"

- Jesus' obedience unto death, even the humiliating death on the cross, was part of His perfecting process.

2. Hebrews 5:8-9: "Son though he was, he learned obedience from what he suffered and, once made perfect, he became the source of eternal salvation for all who obey him."

- Jesus learned obedience through suffering, and through this, He was made perfect, becoming the source of eternal salvation.

Bringing Many Sons and Daughters to Glory

Jesus' role as the pioneer of salvation is not merely about His own perfection but also about leading others to glory.

1. Romans 8:29-30: "For those God foreknew he also predestined to be conformed to the image of his Son, that he might be the firstborn among many brothers and sisters. And those he predestined, he also called; those he called, he also justified; those he justified, he also glorified."

- Jesus, as the firstborn among many brothers and sisters, leads believers through the process of being called, justified, and ultimately glorified.

2. 1 Peter 3:18: "For Christ also suffered once for sins, the righteous for the unrighteous, to bring you to God. He was put to death in the body but made alive in the Spirit."

- Jesus' suffering and death were for the purpose of bringing believers to God, fulfilling His role as the pioneer leading us to salvation and glory.

Expository Study and Strong's Concordance Analysis

Hebrews 2:10 - "In bringing many sons and daughters to glory, it was fitting that God, for whom and through whom everything exists, should make the pioneer of their salvation perfect through what he suffered."

- Pioneer (ἀρχηγός, archēgos): This term refers to a leader, prince, or originator, indicating Jesus as the one who leads the way in salvation.

- Strong's Concordance: G747 – archēgos; a chief leader, author, captain.

- Perfect (τελειῶσαι, teleiōsai): This verb means to complete, finish, or bring to maturity. In the context of Jesus' suffering, it signifies the completion of His mission through His experiences.

- Strong's Concordance: G5048 – teleioō; to make perfect, complete, finish.

- Suffered (παθημάτων, pathēmatōn): This term refers to suffering, particularly enduring hardship or pain. Jesus' sufferings were integral to His perfecting process.

- Strong's Concordance: G3804 – pathēma; suffering, affliction.

Hebrews 5:9 - "And once made perfect, he became the source of eternal salvation for all who obey him."

- Source (αἴτιος, aitios): This term means cause or author, indicating Jesus as the one who initiates and provides salvation.

- Strong's Concordance: G159 – aitios; a cause, author, source.

- Obey (ὑπακούουσιν, hypakouousin): This verb means to listen attentively, to heed, or to conform to a command. Salvation is for those who obey Jesus.

- Strong's Concordance: G5219 – hypakouō; to obey, listen to, be subject to.

Practical Implications for Believers

1. Following the Pioneer: Believers are called to follow Jesus, the pioneer of their salvation. His path of suffering, obedience, and exaltation serves as a model for the Christian life.

2. Enduring Suffering: Understanding that Jesus was perfected through suffering can encourage believers to endure their own trials, knowing that these experiences can lead to spiritual maturity and deeper reliance on God.

3. Living in Obedience: Jesus' role as the pioneer of salvation emphasizes the importance of obedience in the believer's life. Following Jesus means listening to His teachings and living according to His example.

4. Assurance of Salvation: Knowing that Jesus has pioneered the way to salvation provides believers with assurance and confidence. His completed work guarantees that those who follow Him will also be brought to glory.

Conclusion

Hebrews 2:9-18 presents Jesus as the pioneer of salvation, perfected through suffering. By exploring these themes through an expository study and analysis using Strong's Concordance, we gain a deeper understanding of His leading role in our salvation. This understanding enriches our theological knowledge and enhances our faith, guiding us in our relationship with God and our daily walk with Christ.

In the chapters that follow, we will continue to delve into the rich theological insights of Hebrews, drawing lessons that illuminate the significance of Jesus' dual nature and teachings for our lives today.

BROTHERHOOD WITH BELIEVERS

Jesus is Not Ashamed to Call Believers His Brothers and Sisters, Highlighting His Deep Relational Connection with Humanity

Key Verses: Hebrews 2:9-18

"But we do see Jesus, who was made lower than the angels for a little while, now crowned with glory and honor because he suffered death, so that by the grace of God he might taste death for everyone. In bringing many sons and daughters to glory, it was fitting that God, for whom and through whom everything exists, should make the pioneer of their salvation perfect through what he suffered. Both the one who makes people holy and those who are made holy are of the same family. So Jesus is not ashamed to call them brothers and sisters. He says, 'I will declare your name to my brothers and sisters; in the assembly I will sing your praises.' And again, 'I will put my trust in him.' And again he says, 'Here am I, and the children God has given me.' Since the children have flesh and blood, he too shared in their humanity so that by his death he might break the power of him who holds the power of death—that is, the devil—and free those who all their lives were held in slavery by their fear of death. For surely it is not angels he helps, but Abraham's descendants. For this reason he had to be made like them, fully human in every way, in order that he might become a merciful and faithful high priest in service to God, and that he might make atonement for the sins of the people. Because he himself suffered when he was tempted, he is able to help those who are being tempted." (Hebrews 2:9-18, NIV)

Introduction

The book of Hebrews highlights Jesus' deep relational connection with humanity by emphasizing His brotherhood with believers. This chapter explores the theological significance of Jesus calling believers His brothers and sisters, underscoring His full identification with humanity and His intimate relationship with those who follow Him. By examining biblical references and employing an expository study with exhaustive Strong's Concordance, we can gain a deeper understanding of this profound truth.

Jesus' Identification with Humanity

Shared Humanity

Hebrews 2:14-15 emphasizes that Jesus shared in humanity's flesh and blood to fully identify with us and to defeat the power of death.

1. John 1:14: "The Word became flesh and made his dwelling among us. We have seen his glory, the glory of the one and only Son, who came from the Father, full of grace and truth."

- This verse highlights the incarnation of Jesus, where He took on human flesh to live among us, fully identifying with the human experience.

2. Philippians 2:7-8: "Rather, he made himself nothing by taking the very nature of a servant, being made in human likeness. And being found in appearance as a man, he humbled himself by becoming obedient to death—even death on a cross!"

- Jesus' humility and obedience unto death underscore His complete identification with humanity.

Jesus as Brother to Believers

Not Ashamed to Call Them Brothers and Sisters

Hebrews 2:11 declares that Jesus is not ashamed to call believers His brothers and sisters, signifying a profound familial relationship.

1. Matthew 12:49-50: "Pointing to his disciples, he said, 'Here are my mother and my brothers. For whoever does the will of my Father in heaven is my brother and sister and mother.'"

- Jesus explicitly identifies those who follow God's will as His family, reinforcing the concept of spiritual kinship.

2. Romans 8:29: "For those God foreknew he also predestined to be conformed to the image of his Son, that he might be the firstborn among many brothers and sisters."

- Jesus is described as the firstborn among many brothers and sisters, highlighting the familial relationship between Him and believers.

Declaration of God's Name to Believers

Hebrews 2:12 cites Psalm 22:22, where Jesus declares God's name to His brothers and sisters, showing His role in revealing God to humanity.

1. Psalm 22:22: "I will declare your name to my people; in the assembly I will praise you."

- This messianic psalm, fulfilled in Jesus, emphasizes His role in proclaiming God's name to His followers.

2. John 17:26: "I have made you known to them, and will continue to make you known in order that the love you have for me may be in them and that I myself may be in them."

- Jesus' prayer highlights His ongoing work of making God known to believers, deepening their relationship with the Father.

Expository Study and Strong's Concordance Analysis

Hebrews 2:11 - "Both the one who makes people holy and those who are made holy are of the same family. So Jesus is not ashamed to call them brothers and sisters."

- Makes Holy (ἁγιάζων, hagiazōn): This term refers to the process of sanctification, where Jesus makes believers holy.

- Strong's Concordance: G37 – hagiazō; to make holy, consecrate, sanctify.

- Brothers and Sisters (ἀδελφοὺς, adelphous): This term means siblings, indicating a close familial relationship.

- Strong's Concordance: G80 – adelphos; a brother, member of the same family.

Hebrews 2:12 - "He says, 'I will declare your name to my brothers and sisters; in the assembly I will sing your praises.'"

- Declare (ἀπαγγελῶ, apangelō): This verb means to announce or proclaim, indicating Jesus' role in revealing God's name to believers.

- Strong's Concordance: G518 – apangellō; to announce, report.

- Assembly (ἐκκλησίας, ekklēsias): This term refers to the gathering or congregation of believers, emphasizing the communal aspect of worship.

- Strong's Concordance: G1577 – ekklēsia; an assembly, congregation, church.

Theological Significance of Brotherhood with Believers

Shared Humanity and Redemption

Jesus' brotherhood with believers emphasizes His shared humanity and His role in redemption.

1. Hebrews 4:15: "For we do not have a high priest who is unable to empathize with our weaknesses, but we have one who has been tempted in every way, just as we are—yet he did not sin."

- Jesus' ability to empathize with our weaknesses highlights His full identification with humanity and His sinless perfection.

2. Galatians 4:4-5: "But when the set time had fully come, God sent his Son, born of a woman, born under the

law, to redeem those under the law, that we might receive adoption to sonship."

- Jesus' incarnation and redemption work make believers children of God, reinforcing the familial relationship.

Intimate Relationship with Believers

Jesus' willingness to call believers His brothers and sisters underscores His intimate relationship with them.

1. John 15:15: "I no longer call you servants, because a servant does not know his master's business. Instead, I have called you friends, for everything that I learned from my Father I have made known to you."

- This verse highlights the closeness and transparency in Jesus' relationship with His followers.

2. Ephesians 2:19: "Consequently, you are no longer foreigners and strangers, but fellow citizens with God's people and also members of his household."

- Believers are members of God's household, indicating a close familial bond.

Practical Implications for Believers

1. Identity in Christ: Believers can find their true identity in their relationship with Jesus, knowing they are part of His family and are called His brothers and sisters.

2. Confidence in Relationship: Understanding that Jesus is not ashamed to call them His family provides believers with confidence in their relationship with Him, fostering a sense of belonging and acceptance.

3. Call to Holiness: As Jesus makes believers holy, they are called to live in a manner that reflects their new identity, striving for holiness in their daily lives.

4. Strength in Unity: Recognizing the shared brotherhood with Jesus encourages believers to cultivate unity and love within the Christian community, reflecting the relational nature of their faith.

Conclusion

Hebrews 2:9-18 presents a profound insight into Jesus' brotherhood with believers, emphasizing His full identification with humanity and His intimate relationship with those who follow Him. By exploring these themes through an expository study and analysis using Strong's Concordance, we gain a deeper understanding of the significance of Jesus calling believers His brothers and sisters. This understanding enriches our theological knowledge and enhances our faith, guiding us in our relationship with God and our daily walk with Christ.

In the chapters that follow, we will continue to delve into the rich theological insights of Hebrews, drawing lessons

that illuminate the significance of Jesus' dual nature and teachings for our lives today.

DEFEATING DEATH

By His Death, He Destroyed the Devil's Power and Freed Those Who Were Held in Slavery by the Fear of Death

Key Verses: Hebrews 2:14-15

"Since the children have flesh and blood, he too shared in their humanity so that by his death he might break the power of him who holds the power of death—that is, the devil—and free those who all their lives were held in slavery by their fear of death." (Hebrews 2:14-15, NIV)

Introduction

The book of Hebrews articulates the profound truth that through His death, Jesus Christ defeated the power of death held by the devil, liberating humanity from the slavery of the fear of death. This chapter explores the theological significance of this victory over death, examining biblical references and employing an expository study with exhaustive Strong's Concordance to unpack these profound truths.

The Power of Death and the Devil

The Devil's Hold on Death

The devil's power over death is a central theme in understanding the necessity of Christ's sacrifice.

1. Genesis 3:15: "And I will put enmity between you and the woman, and between your offspring and hers; he will crush your head, and you will strike his heel."

- This protoevangelium foreshadows the ultimate defeat of the devil by Jesus, the offspring of the woman.

2. John 8:44: "You belong to your father, the devil, and you want to carry out your father's desires. He was a murderer from the beginning, not holding to the truth, for there is no truth in him."

- The devil is described as a murderer from the beginning, linking his work to death and deception.

3. 1 John 3:8: "The one who does what is sinful is of the devil, because the devil has been sinning from the beginning. The reason the Son of God appeared was to destroy the devil's work."

- This verse clearly states that Jesus came to destroy the works of the devil, including the power of death.

Jesus' Victory Over Death

Death Defeated Through the Cross

Jesus' death on the cross was the pivotal event that broke the devil's power over death.

1. Colossians 2:14-15: "Having canceled the charge of our legal indebtedness, which stood against us and condemned us; he has taken it away, nailing it to the cross.

And having disarmed the powers and authorities, he made a public spectacle of them, triumphing over them by the cross."

- Jesus' crucifixion not only dealt with sin but also disarmed spiritual powers, including the devil.

2. Romans 6:9: "For we know that since Christ was raised from the dead, he cannot die again; death no longer has mastery over him."

- Jesus' resurrection signifies the defeat of death's dominion.

3. 1 Corinthians 15:54-57: "When the perishable has been clothed with the imperishable, and the mortal with immortality, then the saying that is written will come true: 'Death has been swallowed up in victory.' 'Where, O death, is your victory? Where, O death, is your sting?' The sting of death is sin, and the power of sin is the law. But thanks be to God! He gives us the victory through our Lord Jesus Christ."

- This passage celebrates the victory over death and the grave through Jesus Christ.

Liberating Humanity from the Fear of Death

Hebrews 2:15 emphasizes that Jesus' victory frees those who were enslaved by the fear of death.

1. Romans 8:15: "The Spirit you received does not make you slaves, so that you live in fear again; rather, the Spirit

you received brought about your adoption to sonship. And by him, we cry, 'Abba, Father.'"

- Believers are no longer slaves to fear, but children of God, freed by the Spirit of adoption.

2. 2 Timothy 1:10: "But it has now been revealed through the appearing of our Savior, Christ Jesus, who has destroyed death and has brought life and immortality to light through the gospel."

- Jesus' appearance and His work revealed life and immortality, destroying death.

Expository Study and Strong's Concordance Analysis

Hebrews 2:14 - "Since the children have flesh and blood, he too shared in their humanity so that by his death he might break the power of him who holds the power of death—that is, the devil."

- Shared (μετέσχεν, meteschen): This term means to partake or share in something. Jesus shared in humanity by taking on flesh and blood.

- Strong's Concordance: G3348 – metechō; to share, partake of.

- Break (καταργήση, katargēsē): This verb means to render powerless or to nullify. Jesus' death rendered the devil's power over death ineffective.

- Strong's Concordance: G2673 — katargeō; to render idle, inactive, or ineffective.

Hebrews 2:15 - "And free those who all their lives were held in slavery by their fear of death."

- Free (ἀπαλλάξῃ, apallaxē): This term means to release or deliver. Jesus' victory delivers believers from slavery.

- Strong's Concordance: G525 — apallassō; to change, release, deliver.

- Slavery (δουλείας, douleias): This term refers to bondage or servitude. Jesus frees believers from the bondage of fear.

- Strong's Concordance: G1397 — douleia; slavery, bondage.

- Fear (φόβου, phobou): This term means fear or terror. Jesus liberates believers from the terror of death.

- Strong's Concordance: G5401 — phobos; fear, terror, reverence.

Theological Significance of Defeating Death

Jesus' Complete Victory

Jesus' death and resurrection signify His complete victory over death and the devil.

1. Revelation 1:18: "I am the Living One; I was dead, and now look, I am alive for ever and ever! And I hold the keys of death and Hades."

- Jesus' authority over death and Hades confirms His victory.

2. John 11:25-26: "Jesus said to her, 'I am the resurrection and the life. The one who believes in me will live, even though they die; and whoever lives by believing in me will never die. Do you believe this?'"

- Jesus' declaration as the resurrection and life offers believers eternal hope.

Freedom from Fear

Believers are freed from the fear of death, living in the assurance of eternal life.

1. 1 John 4:18: "There is no fear in love. But perfect love drives out fear, because fear has to do with punishment. The one who fears is not made perfect in love."

- Perfect love, manifested in Jesus, drives out the fear of death.

2. Psalm 23:4: "Even though I walk through the darkest valley, I will fear no evil, for you are with me; your rod and your staff, they comfort me."

- The assurance of God's presence removes the fear of death.

Practical Implications for Believers

1. Living Without Fear: Understanding Jesus' victory over death encourages believers to live without the fear of death, trusting in His promise of eternal life.

2. Confidence in Salvation: Jesus' defeat of the devil and death provides believers with confidence in their salvation and the security of their eternal future.

3. Witnessing to Others: The assurance of victory over death empowers believers to share the gospel with boldness, offering hope to those still living in fear.

4. Strength in Trials: Knowing that Jesus has conquered death can provide strength and comfort during trials and sufferings, reinforcing the hope of resurrection and eternal life.

Conclusion

Hebrews 2:14-15 presents a profound insight into Jesus' defeat of death and the devil, emphasizing the liberation of humanity from the fear of death. By exploring these themes through an expository study and analysis using Strong's Concordance, we gain a deeper understanding of the significance of Jesus' victory. This understanding enriches our theological knowledge and enhances our faith, guiding us in our relationship with God and our daily walk with Christ.

In the chapters that follow, we will continue to delve into the rich theological insights of Hebrews, drawing lessons

that illuminate the significance of Jesus' dual nature and teachings for our lives today.

CHAPTER 03

JESUS IS GREATER THAN MOSES

Faithful as a Son: Jesus is Faithful to God as a Son Over God's House, Which Contrasts with Moses Who Was Faithful as a Servant

Key Verses: Hebrews 3:1-6

"Therefore, holy brothers and sisters, who share in the heavenly calling, fix your thoughts on Jesus, whom we acknowledge as our apostle and high priest. He was faithful to the one who appointed him, just as Moses was faithful in all God's house. Jesus has been found worthy of greater honor than Moses, just as the builder of a house has greater honor than the house itself. Every house is built by someone, but God is the builder of everything. 'Moses was faithful as a servant in all God's house,' bearing witness to what would be spoken by God in the future. But Christ is faithful as the Son over God's house. And we are his house, if indeed we hold firmly to our confidence and the hope in which we glory." (Hebrews 3:1-6, NIV)

Introduction

In the book of Hebrews, Jesus is presented as greater than Moses, a key figure in Jewish history and faith. This chapter explores the contrast between Moses' faithfulness as a servant and Jesus' faithfulness as a Son over God's house. By examining biblical references and employing an expository study with exhaustive Strong's Concordance, we can gain a deeper understanding of the significance of Jesus' superior role and faithfulness.

Jesus and Moses: A Comparison

Moses: Faithful as a Servant

Moses is a central figure in the Old Testament, known for leading the Israelites out of Egypt and receiving the Law from God.

1. Numbers 12:7: "But this is not true of my servant Moses; he is faithful in all my house."

- God Himself attests to Moses' faithfulness, acknowledging his unique role and dedication.

2. Deuteronomy 34:10-12: "Since then, no prophet has risen in Israel like Moses, whom the Lord knew face to face, who did all those signs and wonders the Lord sent him to do in Egypt—to Pharaoh and to all his officials and to his whole land. For no one has ever shown the mighty power or performed the awesome deeds that Moses did in the sight of all Israel."

- Moses is celebrated for his close relationship with God and his miraculous works, underscoring his importance and faithfulness.

Jesus: Faithful as a Son

While Moses was a faithful servant, Jesus is presented as a faithful Son, which denotes a higher status and deeper intimacy with God.

1. John 3:35: "The Father loves the Son and has placed everything in his hands."

- This verse emphasizes the unique relationship between the Father and the Son, highlighting Jesus' authority and the Father's love for Him.

2. John 5:19-20: "Jesus gave them this answer: 'Very truly I tell you, the Son can do nothing by himself; he can do only what he sees his Father doing, because whatever the

Father does the Son also does. For the Father loves the Son and shows him all he does. Yes, and he will show him even greater works than these, so that you will be amazed.'"

- Jesus' actions are a direct reflection of the Father's will, indicating His perfect obedience and faithfulness.

3. Matthew 17:5: "While he was still speaking, a bright cloud covered them, and a voice from the cloud said, 'This is my Son, whom I love; with him I am well pleased. Listen to him!'"

- The transfiguration event affirms Jesus' divine sonship and the Father's approval of Him.

Theological Significance of Jesus' Faithfulness

Builder of the House

Hebrews 3:3-4 highlights that Jesus, as the builder of the house, is worthy of greater honor than the house itself.

1. 1 Corinthians 3:11: "For no one can lay any foundation other than the one already laid, which is Jesus Christ."

- Jesus is the foundation and builder of the spiritual house, the church.

2. Ephesians 2:19-22: "Consequently, you are no longer foreigners and strangers, but fellow citizens with God's people and also members of his household, built on the foundation of the apostles and prophets, with Christ Jesus

himself as the chief cornerstone. In him the whole building is joined together and rises to become a holy temple in the Lord."

- Jesus is the cornerstone, and believers are built into a spiritual house, emphasizing His foundational role.

God's House

Hebrews 3:5-6 contrasts Moses' role as a servant in God's house with Jesus' role as a Son over God's house.

1. 1 Peter 2:4-5: "As you come to him, the living Stone—rejected by humans but chosen by God and precious to him—you also, like living stones, are being built into a spiritual house to be a holy priesthood, offering spiritual sacrifices acceptable to God through Jesus Christ."

- Believers are living stones in the spiritual house, with Jesus as the cornerstone, showing the collective aspect of God's house.

2. 1 Timothy 3:15: "If I am delayed, you will know how people ought to conduct themselves in God's household, which is the church of the living God, the pillar and foundation of the truth."

- The church is identified as God's household, with Jesus as its head.

Expository Study and Strong's Concordance Analysis

Hebrews 3:5 - "Moses was faithful as a servant in all God's house."

- Servant (θεράπων, therapōn): This term refers to a servant or attendant, emphasizing Moses' role in serving God's purposes.

- Strong's Concordance: G2324 – therapōn; a minister, servant.

Hebrews 3:6 - "But Christ is faithful as the Son over God's house. And we are his house, if indeed we hold firmly to our confidence and the hope in which we glory."

- Son (υἱός, huios): This term refers to a son, highlighting the familial and authoritative relationship between Jesus and God.

- Strong's Concordance: G5207 – huios; a son.

- House (οἶκος, oikos): This term means house or household, signifying the collective body of believers.

- Strong's Concordance: G3624 – oikos; a house, dwelling, family.

- Hold Firmly (κατάσχωμεν, kataschōmen): This verb means to hold fast or retain, indicating the need for steadfast faith.

- Strong's Concordance: G2722 – katechō; to hold fast, retain.

Practical Implications for Believers

1. Confidence in Jesus' Faithfulness: Believers can have complete confidence in Jesus' faithfulness as the Son over God's house, knowing that He perfectly fulfills His role in leading and sustaining the church.

2. Call to Faithfulness: Just as Moses was faithful as a servant and Jesus as a Son, believers are called to be faithful in their roles within God's house, holding firmly to their confidence and hope in Christ.

3. Identity in God's Household: Understanding their identity as part of God's house can encourage believers to live in unity, purpose, and service, reflecting the values of God's kingdom.

4. Assurance of Hope: The exhortation to hold firmly to confidence and hope underscores the importance of perseverance in the Christian faith, drawing strength from Jesus' example and faithfulness.

Conclusion

Hebrews 3:1-6 presents a profound comparison between Moses and Jesus, emphasizing Jesus' superior role and faithfulness as a Son over God's house. By exploring these themes through an expository study and analysis using Strong's Concordance, we gain a deeper understanding of Jesus' unique relationship with the Father and His preeminent role in the church. This understanding enriches our theological knowledge and enhances our faith, guiding us in our relationship with God and our daily walk with Christ.

In the chapters that follow, we will continue to delve into the rich theological insights of Hebrews, drawing lessons that illuminate the significance of Jesus' dual nature and teachings for our lives today.

BUILDER OF THE HOUSE

While Moses was Part of the House, Jesus is the Builder of the House, Affirming His Superiority and Divine Role in God's Redemptive Plan

Key Verses: Hebrews 3:1-6

"Therefore, holy brothers and sisters, who share in the heavenly calling, fix your thoughts on Jesus, whom we acknowledge as our apostle and high priest. He was faithful to the one who appointed him, just as Moses was faithful in all God's house. Jesus has been found worthy of greater honor than Moses, just as the builder of a house has greater honor than the house itself. For every house is built by someone, but God is the builder of everything. 'Moses was faithful as a servant in all God's house,' bearing witness to what would be spoken by God in the future. But Christ is faithful as the Son over God's house. And we are his house, if indeed we hold firmly to our confidence and the hope in which we glory." (Hebrews 3:1-6, NIV)

Introduction

The book of Hebrews presents a powerful comparison between Moses and Jesus, emphasizing Jesus' superior role as the builder of God's house. This chapter explores the theological significance of Jesus as the builder, examining biblical references and employing an expository study with exhaustive Strong's Concordance. Understanding Jesus' role as the builder of the house affirms His superiority and divine role in God's redemptive plan.

Jesus, the Builder of the House

Moses: Part of the House

Moses is acknowledged as a faithful servant in God's house, but he is part of the house rather than its builder.

1. Numbers 12:7: "But this is not true of my servant Moses; he is faithful in all my house."

- God recognizes Moses' faithfulness in His house, underscoring his significant but limited role.

2. Deuteronomy 34:10-12: "Since then, no prophet has risen in Israel like Moses, whom the Lord knew face to face, who did all those signs and wonders the Lord sent him to do in Egypt—to Pharaoh and to all his officials and to his whole land. For no one has ever shown the mighty power or performed the awesome deeds that Moses did in the sight of all Israel."

- Moses is celebrated for his unique relationship with God and his role in Israel's history, yet he remains part of the house, not its builder.

Jesus: Builder of the House

Jesus is presented as the builder of the house, a role that signifies His divine authority and preeminence.

1. 1 Corinthians 3:11: "For no one can lay any foundation other than the one already laid, which is Jesus Christ."

- Jesus is the foundation and builder of the spiritual house, the church.

2. Ephesians 2:19-22: "Consequently, you are no longer foreigners and strangers, but fellow citizens with God's people and also members of his household, built on the foundation of the apostles and prophets, with Christ Jesus himself as the chief cornerstone. In him the whole building is joined together and rises to become a holy temple in the Lord."

- Jesus is the cornerstone, and believers are built into a spiritual house, emphasizing His foundational role.

3. Matthew 16:18: "And I tell you that you are Peter, and on this rock I will build my church, and the gates of Hades will not overcome it."

- Jesus explicitly states that He will build His church, affirming His role as the builder.

Theological Significance of Jesus as the Builder

Superiority Over Moses

Hebrews 3:3-4 highlights that Jesus, as the builder of the house, is worthy of greater honor than the house itself.

1. John 1:17: "For the law was given through Moses; grace and truth came through Jesus Christ."

- While Moses brought the law, Jesus brought grace and truth, underscoring His superior role in God's redemptive plan.

2. John 8:58: "Very truly I tell you," Jesus answered, "before Abraham was born, I am!"

- Jesus' preexistence and divine identity affirm His superiority over all patriarchs, including Moses.

Divine Role in Redemption

Jesus' role as the builder of the house signifies His divine authority and active participation in God's redemptive plan.

1. Hebrews 12:2: "Fixing our eyes on Jesus, the pioneer and perfecter of faith. For the joy set before him he endured the cross, scorning its shame, and sat down at the right hand of the throne of God."

- Jesus, as the pioneer and perfecter of faith, plays a central role in the redemption and sanctification of believers.

2. Colossians 1:16-17: "For in him all things were created: things in heaven and on earth, visible and invisible, whether thrones or powers or rulers or authorities; all things have been created through him and for him. He is before all things, and in him all things hold together."

- Jesus is not only the builder but also the sustainer of all creation, highlighting His divine authority and role in the cosmos.

Expository Study and Strong's Concordance Analysis

Hebrews 3:3 - "Jesus has been found worthy of greater honor than Moses, just as the builder of a house has greater honor than the house itself."

- Builder (κατασκευάσας, kataskeuasas): This term refers to the one who constructs or prepares something. Jesus, as the builder, is responsible for the creation and sustenance of the house.

- Strong's Concordance: G2680 – kataskeuazō; to prepare, build, construct.

Hebrews 3:4 - "For every house is built by someone, but God is the builder of everything."

- Built (κατασκευάζεται, kataskeuazetai): This verb signifies the act of constructing or preparing something. It reinforces the idea that while humans may build, God is ultimately the supreme builder.

- Strong's Concordance: G2680 – kataskeuazō; to prepare, build, construct.

- Builder (κατασκευάσας, kataskeuasas): This term emphasizes that God, and by extension Jesus, is the ultimate builder of everything.

- Strong's Concordance: G2680 – kataskeuazō; to prepare, build, construct.

Practical Implications for Believers

1. Confidence in Jesus' Authority: Believers can have complete confidence in Jesus' authority as the builder of God's house, knowing that He has the divine power to build and sustain the church.

2. Role in God's House: Understanding that Jesus is the builder encourages believers to find their place within God's house, contributing to its growth and stability through their gifts and service.

3. Unity and Purpose: Recognizing Jesus as the builder fosters unity among believers, as they acknowledge their shared foundation and purpose in Him.

4. Assurance of Hope: The knowledge that Jesus is actively building His church provides believers with assurance and hope, even in the face of challenges and opposition.

Conclusion

Hebrews 3:1-6 presents a profound comparison between Moses and Jesus, emphasizing Jesus' superior role as the builder of God's house. By exploring these themes through an expository study and analysis using Strong's Concordance, we gain a deeper understanding of Jesus' unique relationship with the Father and His preeminent role in the church. This understanding enriches our theological knowledge and enhances our faith, guiding us in our relationship with God and our daily walk with Christ.

In the chapters that follow, we will continue to delve into the rich theological insights of Hebrews, drawing lessons that illuminate the significance of Jesus' dual nature and teachings for our lives today.

CHAPTER 04

THE REST OF GOD AND THE LIVING WORD

Entering God's Rest: Believers are Encouraged to Strive to Enter God's Rest, Which is Achieved Through Faith in Jesus

Key Verses: Hebrews 4:12-16

"For the word of God is alive and active. Sharper than any double-edged sword, it penetrates even to dividing soul and spirit, joints and marrow; it judges the thoughts and attitudes of the heart. Nothing in all creation is hidden from God's sight. Everything is uncovered and laid bare before the eyes of him to whom we must give account. Therefore, since we have a great high priest who has ascended into heaven, Jesus the Son of God, let us hold firmly to the faith we profess. For we do not have a high priest who is unable to feel sympathy for our weaknesses, but we have one who has been tempted in every way, just as we are—yet he did not sin. Let us then approach God's throne of grace with confidence, so that we may receive mercy and find grace to help us in our time of need." (Hebrews 4:12-16, NIV)

Introduction

The concept of entering God's rest is a central theme in the book of Hebrews. This chapter explores the significance of this rest, which is achieved through faith in Jesus Christ. By examining biblical references and employing an expository study with exhaustive Strong's Concordance, we can gain a deeper understanding of the rest that God offers and how believers are encouraged to strive to enter it.

Understanding God's Rest

Biblical Foundation

The idea of God's rest originates from the creation narrative and is further developed throughout Scripture.

1. Genesis 2:2-3: "By the seventh day God had finished the work he had been doing; so on the seventh day he rested from all his work. Then God blessed the seventh

day and made it holy, because on it he rested from all the work of creating that he had done."

- God's rest on the seventh day sets a pattern for the Sabbath and introduces the concept of divine rest.

2. Exodus 20:8-11: "Remember the Sabbath day by keeping it holy. Six days you shall labor and do all your work, but the seventh day is a sabbath to the Lord your God. On it you shall not do any work... For in six days the Lord made the heavens and the earth, the sea, and all that is in them, but he rested on the seventh day. Therefore the Lord blessed the Sabbath day and made it holy."

- The Sabbath rest for Israel is a reflection of God's rest, meant to be a time of cessation from labor and dedication to God.

The Promised Land as a Type of Rest

The journey of the Israelites to the Promised Land serves as a foreshadowing of the ultimate rest that believers find in Christ.

1. Deuteronomy 12:9: "Since you have not yet reached the resting place and the inheritance the Lord your God is giving you."

- The Promised Land is described as a resting place for Israel, symbolizing a physical and spiritual rest provided by God.

2. Joshua 21:44: "The Lord gave them rest on every side, just as he had sworn to their ancestors. Not one of their enemies withstood them; the Lord gave all their enemies into their hands."

- The fulfillment of God's promise of rest in the land of Canaan points to a greater spiritual rest.

Striving to Enter God's Rest

Faith and Obedience

Entering God's rest is contingent upon faith and obedience to God's Word.

1. Hebrews 3:18-19: "And to whom did God swear that they would never enter his rest if not to those who disobeyed? So we see that they were not able to enter, because of their unbelief."

- Disobedience and unbelief prevented the Israelites from entering God's rest, serving as a warning to believers.

2. Hebrews 4:1-2: "Therefore, since the promise of entering his rest still stands, let us be careful that none of you be found to have fallen short of it. For we also have had the good news proclaimed to us, just as they did; but the message they heard was of no value to them, because they did not share the faith of those who obeyed."

- The promise of rest remains, and believers are encouraged to combine faith with obedience to enter it.

The Role of Jesus

Jesus, as the ultimate high priest, is central to the believer's ability to enter God's rest.

1. Hebrews 4:14-16: "Therefore, since we have a great high priest who has ascended into heaven, Jesus the Son of God, let us hold firmly to the faith we profess. For we do not have a high priest who is unable to feel sympathy for our weaknesses, but we have one who has been tempted in every way, just as we are—yet he did not sin. Let us then approach God's throne of grace with confidence, so that we may receive mercy and find grace to help us in our time of need."

- Jesus' role as high priest provides believers with the confidence to approach God and receive the necessary grace and mercy to strive towards entering His rest.

Expository Study and Strong's Concordance Analysis

Hebrews 4:1 - "Therefore, since the promise of entering his rest still stands, let us be careful that none of you be found to have fallen short of it."

- Rest (κατάπαυσιν, katapausin): This term refers to a cessation or a place of rest. It is used here to describe the spiritual rest that God offers.

- Strong's Concordance: G2663 — katapausis; a resting place, rest.

- Fallen Short (ὑστερηκέναι, husterēkenai): This verb means to come short or to lack. Believers are warned not to fall short of the promise of entering God's rest.

- Strong's Concordance: G5302 — hustereō; to come late, be behind, lack, come short.

Hebrews 4:11 - "Let us, therefore, make every effort to enter that rest, so that no one will perish by following their example of disobedience."

- Make Every Effort (σπουδάσωμεν, spoudasōmen): This verb means to strive or to be diligent. Believers are encouraged to exert themselves to enter God's rest.

- Strong's Concordance: G4704 — spoudazō; to make haste, be diligent, exert oneself.

- Disobedience (ἀπειθείας, apeitheias): This term refers to unbelief or disobedience. It highlights the reason why some failed to enter God's rest.

- Strong's Concordance: G543 — apeitheia; disbelief, obstinate, rebellion.

Practical Implications for Believers

1. Faith and Obedience: Believers are called to combine faith with obedience to enter God's rest. Trusting in

God's promises and living according to His Word are essential.

2. Confidence in Christ: Jesus' role as high priest provides believers with the confidence to approach God's throne of grace, ensuring that they can find the help they need to strive towards entering God's rest.

3. Avoiding Unbelief: The example of the Israelites' unbelief serves as a warning. Believers are encouraged to remain steadfast in faith to avoid falling short of the promise.

4. Experiencing Spiritual Rest: Entering God's rest involves a spiritual dimension where believers find peace and cessation from striving, resting in the completed work of Christ.

Conclusion

Hebrews 4:12-16 presents a profound insight into the concept of entering God's rest, emphasizing the need for faith and obedience. By exploring these themes through an expository study and analysis using Strong's Concordance, we gain a deeper understanding of the rest that God offers and how believers can strive to enter it through faith in Jesus Christ. This understanding enriches our theological knowledge and enhances our faith, guiding us in our relationship with God and our daily walk with Christ.

In the chapters that follow, we will continue to delve into the rich theological insights of Hebrews, drawing lessons that illuminate the significance of Jesus' dual nature and teachings for our lives today.

LIVING WORD

The Word of God, Embodied in Jesus, is Alive, Active, and Sharper than Any Double-Edged Sword, Able to Judge Thoughts and Attitudes

Key Verses: Hebrews 4:12-16

"For the word of God is alive and active. Sharper than any double-edged sword, it penetrates even to dividing soul and spirit, joints and marrow; it judges the thoughts and attitudes of the heart. Nothing in all creation is hidden from God's sight. Everything is uncovered and laid bare before the eyes of him to whom we must give account. Therefore, since we have a great high priest who has ascended into heaven, Jesus the Son of God, let us hold firmly to the faith we profess. For we do not have a high priest who is unable to feel sympathy for our weaknesses, but we have one who has been tempted in every way, just as we are—yet he did not sin. Let us then approach God's throne of grace with confidence, so that we may receive mercy and find grace to help us in our time of need." (Hebrews 4:12-16, NIV)

Introduction

The book of Hebrews emphasizes the dynamic nature of the Word of God, portraying it as living, active, and penetrating. This chapter explores the theological significance of the Living Word, embodied in Jesus, and its power to judge the thoughts and attitudes of the heart. By examining biblical references and employing an expository study with exhaustive Strong's Concordance, we can gain a deeper understanding of the Living Word's role in the life of believers.

The Living Word

The Word of God as Alive and Active

Hebrews 4:12 describes the Word of God as living and active, indicating its dynamic and powerful nature.

1. John 1:1-4: "In the beginning was the Word, and the Word was with God, and the Word was God. He was with God in the beginning. Through him all things were made; without him nothing was made that has been made. In him was life, and that life was the light of all mankind."

- Jesus is identified as the Word, emphasizing His divine nature and active role in creation and revelation.

2. Isaiah 55:11: "So is my word that goes out from my mouth: It will not return to me empty but will accomplish what I desire and achieve the purpose for which I sent it."

- God's Word is effective and accomplishes His purposes, reflecting its living and active nature.

The Word of God as Sharp and Penetrating

The Word of God is depicted as sharper than any double-edged sword, able to penetrate deeply.

1. Ephesians 6:17: "Take the helmet of salvation and the sword of the Spirit, which is the word of God."

- The Word of God is likened to a sword, emphasizing its power to penetrate and discern.

2. Revelation 1:16: "In his right hand he held seven stars, and coming out of his mouth was a sharp, double-edged sword. His face was like the sun shining in all its brilliance."

- The imagery of the sharp, double-edged sword coming from Jesus' mouth highlights the penetrating power of His Word.

The Word of God as Judge

Hebrews 4:12-13 emphasizes the Word's ability to judge the thoughts and attitudes of the heart, laying everything bare before God.

1. Psalm 139:23-24: "Search me, God, and know my heart; test me and know my anxious thoughts. See if there is any offensive way in me, and lead me in the way everlasting."

- The psalmist invites God to examine his heart, reflecting the judging and discerning role of God's Word.

2. 1 Corinthians 14:24-25: "But if an unbeliever or an inquirer comes in while everyone is prophesying, they are

convicted of sin and are brought under judgment by all, as the secrets of their hearts are laid bare. So they will fall down and worship God, exclaiming, 'God is really among you!'"

- The prophetic Word of God reveals the secrets of the heart, leading to conviction and worship.

Expository Study and Strong's Concordance Analysis

Hebrews 4:12 - "For the word of God is alive and active. Sharper than any double-edged sword, it penetrates even to dividing soul and spirit, joints and marrow; it judges the thoughts and attitudes of the heart."

- Alive (ζῶν, zōn): This term signifies being alive or living, indicating the dynamic and ongoing life inherent in the Word of God.

- Strong's Concordance: G2198 – zaō; to live, be alive.

- Active (ἐνεργής, energēs): This term means active or effective, highlighting the powerful and effective nature of the Word.

- Strong's Concordance: G1756 – energēs; active, powerful, effective.

- Sharper (τομώτερος, tomōteros): This term means sharper, indicating the ability of the Word to cut deeply and precisely.

- Strong's Concordance: G5114 – tomōteros; sharper, more cutting.

- Penetrates (διϊκνούμενος, diiknoumenos): This verb means to penetrate or pierce through, emphasizing the deep and thorough impact of the Word.

- Strong's Concordance: G1338 – diikneomai; to go through, penetrate.

- Judges (κριτικὸς, kritikos): This term refers to being able to judge or discern, highlighting the discerning nature of the Word.

- Strong's Concordance: G2924 – kritikos; decisive, able to judge.

Hebrews 4:13 - "Nothing in all creation is hidden from God's sight. Everything is uncovered and laid bare before the eyes of him to whom we must give account."

- Hidden (ἀφανὴς, aphanes): This term means hidden or concealed, indicating that nothing is hidden from God's sight.

- Strong's Concordance: G852 – aphanes; unseen, hidden.

- Uncovered (γυμνὰ, gymna): This term means naked or exposed, indicating complete openness before God.

- Strong's Concordance: G1131 – gymnos; naked, bare.

- Laid Bare (τετραχηλισμένα, tetrachēlismena): This term means to be laid bare or exposed, emphasizing the thorough exposure before God.

- Strong's Concordance: G5136 – trachēlizō; to expose, lay bare.

Practical Implications for Believers

1. Engaging with the Living Word: Believers are called to actively engage with the Word of God, recognizing its dynamic and life-giving power. Regular reading, meditation, and application of Scripture are essential.

2. Allowing the Word to Penetrate: Understanding the sharp and penetrating nature of the Word, believers should allow it to deeply examine and transform their hearts and minds, leading to genuine spiritual growth.

3. Submitting to God's Judgment: Recognizing that the Word judges thoughts and attitudes, believers should live transparently before God, inviting His Word to reveal and correct any hidden sin or wrong motives.

4. Confidence in Christ's Role: Knowing that Jesus, the Living Word, is also the high priest who sympathizes with our weaknesses, believers can approach God's throne of grace with confidence, receiving mercy and grace in times of need.

Conclusion

Hebrews 4:12-16 presents a profound insight into the nature of the Word of God, emphasizing its living, active, and penetrating power. By exploring these themes through an expository study and analysis using Strong's Concordance, we gain a deeper understanding of the Living Word's role in judging the thoughts and attitudes of the heart. This understanding enriches our theological knowledge and enhances our faith, guiding us in our relationship with God and our daily walk with Christ.

In the chapters that follow, we will continue to delve into the rich theological insights of Hebrews, drawing lessons that illuminate the significance of Jesus' dual nature and teachings for our lives today.

SYMPATHETIC HIGH PRIEST

Sympathetic High Priest: Jesus, Our Great High Priest, Sympathizes with Our Weaknesses, Having Been Tempted in Every Way, Yet Without Sin, Enabling Us to Approach the Throne of Grace with Confidence

Key Verses: Hebrews 4:14-16

"Therefore, since we have a great high priest who has ascended into heaven, Jesus the Son of God, let us hold firmly to the faith we profess. For we do not have a high priest who is unable to feel sympathy for our weaknesses, but we have one who has been tempted in every way, just as we are—yet he did not sin. Let us then approach God's throne of grace with confidence, so that we may receive mercy and find grace to help us in our time of need." (Hebrews 4:14-16, NIV)

Introduction

The book of Hebrews portrays Jesus as the sympathetic high priest who understands our weaknesses and provides believers with the confidence to approach God's throne of grace. This chapter explores the theological significance of Jesus' high priesthood, emphasizing His empathy, sinlessness, and the implications for believers. By examining biblical references and employing an expository study with exhaustive Strong's Concordance, we can gain a deeper understanding of the compassionate nature of Jesus' priesthood.

Jesus as the Great High Priest

Ascended into Heaven

Hebrews 4:14 highlights that Jesus, our great high priest, has ascended into heaven, underscoring His divine authority and eternal priesthood.

1. Hebrews 7:24-25: "But because Jesus lives forever, he has a permanent priesthood. Therefore he is able to save completely those who come to God through him, because he always lives to intercede for them."

- Jesus' eternal priesthood ensures that He continually intercedes for believers, providing ongoing access to God.

2. Hebrews 9:24: "For Christ did not enter a sanctuary made with human hands that was only a copy of the true one; he entered heaven itself, now to appear for us in God's presence."

- Jesus' ascension into heaven signifies His entry into the true sanctuary, where He represents believers before God.

Sympathizes with Our Weaknesses

Hebrews 4:15 emphasizes Jesus' empathy, stating that He sympathizes with our weaknesses because He has been tempted in every way, yet without sin.

1. Isaiah 53:3-4: "He was despised and rejected by mankind, a man of suffering, and familiar with pain. Like one from whom people hide their faces he was despised, and we held him in low esteem. Surely he took up our pain and bore our suffering, yet we considered him punished by God, stricken by him, and afflicted."

- The prophetic description of the suffering servant highlights Jesus' experience of human suffering and His empathetic nature.

2. Matthew 4:1-11: The account of Jesus' temptation in the wilderness demonstrates that He faced real temptations, enabling Him to empathize with our struggles.

3. 2 Corinthians 5:21: "God made him who had no sin to be sin for us, so that in him we might become the righteousness of God."

- Despite being without sin, Jesus took on the consequences of sin, showcasing His profound empathy and sacrificial love.

Expository Study and Strong's Concordance Analysis

Hebrews 4:15 - "For we do not have a high priest who is unable to feel sympathy for our weaknesses, but we have one who has been tempted in every way, just as we are—yet he did not sin."

- Sympathy (συμπαθῆσαι, sympathe□ sai): This term means to feel sympathy or compassion. It highlights Jesus' ability to empathize with human weaknesses.

- Strong's Concordance: G4834 — sympatheō; to feel compassion, to sympathize.

- Weaknesses (ἀσθενείαις, astheneiais): This term refers to weaknesses or infirmities. It indicates the human frailties that Jesus understands.

- Strong's Concordance: G769 — astheneia; weakness, infirmity, feebleness.

- Tempted (πειρασθέντα, peirasthe□nta): This verb means to be tried or tested. It underscores that Jesus experienced temptation.

- Strong's Concordance: G3985 – peirazō; to test, to try, to tempt.

- Without Sin (χωρὶς ἁμαρτίας, chōris hamartias): This phrase signifies being free from sin, highlighting Jesus' sinlessness despite facing temptation.

- Strong's Concordance: G5565 – chōris; separately, apart from.

- Strong's Concordance: G266 – hamartia; sin, wrongdoing.

Hebrews 4:16 - "Let us then approach God's throne of grace with confidence, so that we may receive mercy and find grace to help us in our time of need."

- Approach (προσερχώμεθα, proserchōmetha): This verb means to draw near or come forward. Believers are encouraged to confidently approach God.

- Strong's Concordance: G4334 – proserchomai; to come near, to approach.

- Confidence (παρρησίας, parrēsias): This term means boldness or confidence. It reflects the assurance believers have in approaching God.

- Strong's Concordance: G3954 — parrēsia; boldness, confidence, openness.

- Mercy (ἔλεος, eleos): This term refers to compassion or mercy. Believers receive God's mercy through Jesus.

- Strong's Concordance: G1656 — eleos; mercy, compassion, pity.

- Grace (χάριν, charin): This term means grace or favor. Believers find grace to help them in times of need.

- Strong's Concordance: G5485 — charis; grace, favor, kindness.

Theological Significance of Jesus as the Sympathetic High Priest

Empathy and Identification

Jesus' ability to sympathize with human weaknesses is a profound aspect of His priesthood.

1. Philippians 2:6-8: "Who, being in very nature God, did not consider equality with God something to be used to his own advantage; rather, he made himself nothing by taking the very nature of a servant, being made in human likeness. And being found in appearance as a man, he humbled himself by becoming obedient to death—even death on a cross!"

- Jesus' incarnation and humility demonstrate His identification with humanity and His empathetic nature.

2. Romans 8:3: "For what the law was powerless to do because it was weakened by the flesh, God did by sending his own Son in the likeness of sinful flesh to be a sin offering. And so he condemned sin in the flesh."

- Jesus came in the likeness of sinful flesh, experiencing human weakness, yet without sin.

Access to God's Grace and Mercy

Jesus' priesthood provides believers with confident access to God's throne of grace.

1. Ephesians 3:12: "In him and through faith in him we may approach God with freedom and confidence."

- Believers have the freedom and confidence to approach God through faith in Jesus.

2. Hebrews 10:19-22: "Therefore, brothers and sisters, since we have confidence to enter the Most Holy Place by the blood of Jesus, by a new and living way opened for us through the curtain, that is, his body, and since we have a great priest over the house of God, let us draw near to God with a sincere heart and with the full assurance that faith brings, having our hearts sprinkled to cleanse us from a guilty conscience and having our bodies washed with pure water."

- The sacrificial work of Jesus allows believers to draw near to God with a cleansed conscience and full assurance.

Practical Implications for Believers

1. Confidence in Prayer: Believers are encouraged to approach God's throne of grace with confidence, knowing that Jesus understands their struggles and intercedes for them.

2. Receiving Mercy and Grace: Understanding that Jesus empathizes with their weaknesses, believers can receive mercy and find grace to help them in their times of need.

3. Living Transparently: Recognizing that nothing is hidden from God's sight, believers are called to live transparently, inviting God to examine and transform their hearts.

4. Perseverance in Faith: Holding firmly to the faith they profess, believers are inspired to persevere, knowing that their high priest, Jesus, has overcome every temptation and remains sinless.

Conclusion

Hebrews 4:14-16 presents a profound insight into the sympathetic nature of Jesus as the high priest, emphasizing His empathy and sinlessness. By exploring these themes through an expository study and analysis using Strong's Concordance, we gain a deeper understanding of the compassionate nature of Jesus' priesthood. This understanding enriches our theological knowledge and enhances our faith, guiding us in our relationship with God and our daily walk with Christ.

In the chapters that follow, we will continue to delve into the rich theological insights of Hebrews, drawing lessons that illuminate the significance of Jesus' dual nature and teachings for our lives today.

CHAPTER 05

THE HIGH PRIESTHOOD OF JESUS

Appointed by God: Jesus Did Not Glorify Himself but Was Appointed by God as a High Priest in the Order of Melchizedek

Key Verses: Hebrews 5:1-10

"Every high priest is selected from among the people and is appointed to represent the people in matters related to God, to offer gifts and sacrifices for sins. He is able to deal gently with those who are ignorant and are going astray since he himself is subject to weakness. This is why he has to offer sacrifices for his own sins, as well as for the sins of the people.

And no one takes this honor on himself, but he receives it when called by God, just as Aaron was. In the same way, Christ did not take on himself the glory of becoming a high priest. But God said to him, 'You are my Son; today I have become your Father.' And he says in another place, 'You are a priest forever, in the order of Melchizedek.' During the days of Jesus' life on earth, he offered up prayers and petitions with fervent cries and tears to the one who could save him from death, and he was heard because of his reverent submission. Son though he was, he learned obedience from what he suffered and, once made perfect, he became the source of eternal salvation for all who obey him and was designated by God to be high priest in the order of Melchizedek." (Hebrews 5:1-10, NIV)

Introduction

The book of Hebrews presents Jesus as a high priest appointed by God, not by human aspiration or self-glorification. This chapter explores the theological significance of Jesus' divine appointment as a high priest in the order of Melchizedek, emphasizing the unique aspects of His priesthood and its implications for believers. By examining biblical references and employing an expository study with exhaustive Strong's Concordance, we can gain a deeper understanding of Jesus' priesthood and its foundational role in the Christian faith.

The Nature of the High Priesthood

Human High Priests

High priests in the Old Testament were appointed to represent the people before God and offer sacrifices for sins.

1. Exodus 28:1: "Have Aaron your brother brought to you from among the Israelites, along with his sons Nadab and Abihu, Eleazar and Ithamar, so they may serve me as priests."

- Aaron and his descendants were appointed by God to serve as priests, emphasizing divine selection.

2. Leviticus 16:32-34: "The priest who is anointed and ordained to succeed his father as high priest is to make atonement. He is to put on the sacred linen garments and make atonement for the Most Holy Place, for the tent of meeting and the altar, and for the priests and all the members of the community."

- The high priest's role in making atonement highlights the gravity and responsibility of the position.

Jesus as the High Priest

Jesus' high priesthood is distinct in that it is eternal and in the order of Melchizedek, rather than Aaron.

1. Psalm 110:4: "The Lord has sworn and will not change his mind: 'You are a priest forever, in the order of Melchizedek.'"

- This messianic psalm predicts an eternal priesthood in the order of Melchizedek, fulfilled in Jesus.

2. Hebrews 7:17: "For it is declared: 'You are a priest forever, in the order of Melchizedek.'"

- The repetition of this declaration in Hebrews reinforces Jesus' unique and eternal priesthood.

Appointed by God

Divine Appointment

Jesus did not glorify Himself but was appointed by God as a high priest, underscoring the divine origin and legitimacy of His priesthood.

1. John 8:54: "Jesus replied, 'If I glorify myself, my glory means nothing. My Father, whom you claim as your God, is the one who glorifies me.'"

- Jesus acknowledges that His glory and appointment come from the Father, not from self-exaltation.

2. Philippians 2:9: "Therefore God exalted him to the highest place and gave him the name that is above every name."

- God's exaltation of Jesus signifies His divine appointment and authority.

High Priest in the Order of Melchizedek

Jesus' priesthood is modeled after Melchizedek, a unique figure in the Old Testament who combined kingship and priesthood.

1. Genesis 14:18-20: "Then Melchizedek king of Salem brought out bread and wine. He was priest of God Most High, and he blessed Abram, saying, 'Blessed be Abram by God Most High, Creator of heaven and earth. And praise be to God Most High, who delivered your enemies into your hand.' Then Abram gave him a tenth of everything."

- Melchizedek's dual role as king and priest prefigures Jesus' eternal and royal priesthood.

2. Hebrews 7:1-3: "This Melchizedek was king of Salem and priest of God Most High. He met Abraham returning from the defeat of the kings and blessed him, and Abraham gave him a tenth of everything. First, the name Melchizedek means 'king of righteousness'; then also, 'king of Salem' means 'king of peace.' Without father or mother, without genealogy, without beginning of days or end of life, resembling the Son of God, he remains a priest forever."

- Melchizedek's lack of genealogy and eternal priesthood serve as a typology for Jesus' eternal priesthood.

Expository Study and Strong's Concordance Analysis

Hebrews 5:5 - "In the same way, Christ did not take on himself the glory of becoming a high priest. But God said to him, 'You are my Son; today I have become your Father.'"

- Glory (δόξαν, doxan): This term refers to honor or splendor. Jesus did not seek self-glorification; His honor was conferred by God.

- Strong's Concordance: G1391 – doxa; glory, honor, splendor.

- Appointed (ἐγεννήθης, egenne☐ the☐ s): This verb means to beget or bring forth. God's declaration signifies Jesus' divine appointment.

- Strong's Concordance: G1080 – gennaō; to beget, to bring forth.

Hebrews 5:10 - "And was designated by God to be high priest in the order of Melchizedek."

- Designated (προσαγορευθεὶς, prosagoreutheis): This term means to be addressed or designated. Jesus' appointment as high priest is formally recognized by God.

- Strong's Concordance: G4316 – prosagoreuō; to address, to designate.

- Order (τάξιν, taxin): This term refers to arrangement or order. Jesus' priesthood follows the unique order of Melchizedek.

- Strong's Concordance: G5010 – taxis; order, arrangement.

Theological Significance of Jesus' Appointment

Eternal Priesthood

Jesus' priesthood is eternal, surpassing the temporal priesthood of Aaron.

1. Hebrews 7:23-24: "Now there have been many of those priests, since death prevented them from continuing in office; but because Jesus lives forever, he has a permanent priesthood."

- The eternal nature of Jesus' priesthood provides perpetual intercession for believers.

Perfect Sacrifice

Jesus, as high priest, offers Himself as the perfect sacrifice, fulfilling and surpassing the old sacrificial system.

1. Hebrews 9:11-12: "But when Christ came as high priest of the good things that are now already here, he went through the greater and more perfect tabernacle that is not made with human hands, that is to say, is not a part of this creation. He did not enter by means of the blood of goats and calves; but he entered the Most Holy Place once for all by his own blood, thus obtaining eternal redemption."

- Jesus' self-sacrifice secures eternal redemption, contrasting with the repeated sacrifices of the old covenant.

Mediator of the New Covenant

Jesus' priesthood mediates a new and better covenant between God and humanity.

1. Hebrews 8:6: "But in fact the ministry Jesus has received is as superior to theirs as the covenant of which he is mediator is superior to the old one, since the new covenant is established on better promises."

- Jesus mediates a superior covenant, offering better promises and a more profound relationship with God.

Practical Implications for Believers

1. Confidence in Salvation: Believers can have complete confidence in their salvation, knowing that Jesus, appointed by God, intercedes for them eternally as their high priest.

2. Understanding of Priesthood: Recognizing Jesus as the high priest in the order of Melchizedek helps believers understand the fulfillment and transcendence of the old covenant's priesthood.

3. Approaching God Boldly: Believers are encouraged to approach God's throne of grace with confidence, assured of Jesus' ongoing intercession and the efficacy of His sacrifice.

4. Living in the New Covenant: Embracing the new covenant mediated by Jesus, believers are called to live in the

fullness of its promises, experiencing a deeper and more intimate relationship with God.

Conclusion

Hebrews 5:1-10 presents a profound insight into the divine appointment of Jesus as the

high priest in the order of Melchizedek, emphasizing His unique and eternal priesthood. By exploring these themes through an expository study and analysis using Strong's Concordance, we gain a deeper understanding of Jesus' role and its significance for believers. This understanding enriches our theological knowledge and enhances our faith, guiding us in our relationship with God and our daily walk with Christ.

In the chapters that follow, we will continue to delve into the rich theological insights of Hebrews, drawing lessons that illuminate the significance of Jesus' dual nature and teachings for our lives today.

LEARNED OBEDIENCE

Through Suffering, Jesus Learned Obedience and Was Made Perfect, Becoming the Source of Eternal Salvation for All Who Obey Him

Key Verses: Hebrews 5:7-10

"During the days of Jesus' life on earth, he offered up prayers and petitions with fervent cries and tears to the one who could save him from death, and he was heard because of his reverent submission. Son though he was, he learned obedience from what he suffered and, once made perfect, he became the source of eternal salvation for all who obey him and was designated by God to be high priest in the order of Melchizedek." (Hebrews 5:7-10, NIV)

Introduction

The concept of Jesus learning obedience through suffering is a profound theological insight found in the book of Hebrews. This chapter explores the significance of Jesus' learned obedience, how it relates to His perfection, and its implications for believers. By examining biblical references and employing an expository study with exhaustive Strong's Concordance, we can gain a deeper understanding of the process through which Jesus became the source of eternal salvation.

The Human Experience of Jesus

Prayers and Petitions

During His earthly life, Jesus demonstrated deep reliance on God through fervent prayers and petitions, especially in moments of suffering.

1. Luke 22:41-44: "He withdrew about a stone's throw beyond them, knelt down and prayed, 'Father, if you are willing, take this cup from me; yet not my will, but yours be done.' An angel from heaven appeared to him and

strengthened him. And being in anguish, he prayed more earnestly, and his sweat was like drops of blood falling to the ground."

- Jesus' prayer in Gethsemane illustrates His intense struggle and submission to God's will.

2. Matthew 27:46: "About three in the afternoon Jesus cried out in a loud voice, 'Eli, Eli, lema sabachthani?' (which means 'My God, my God, why have you forsaken me?')"

- Jesus' cry on the cross highlights His experience of human suffering and abandonment, yet His trust in God remains.

Learned Obedience Through Suffering

The Nature of Obedience

Hebrews 5:8 states that Jesus, though He was a Son, learned obedience through what He suffered.

1. Philippians 2:8: "And being found in appearance as a man, he humbled himself by becoming obedient to death— even death on a cross!"

- Jesus' humility and obedience unto death demonstrate the extent of His submission to God's will.

2. Isaiah 50:5-7: "The Sovereign Lord has opened my ears; I have not been rebellious, I have not turned away. I offered my back to those who beat me, my cheeks to those who pulled out my beard; I did not hide my face from

mocking and spitting. Because the Sovereign Lord helps me, I will not be disgraced. Therefore have I set my face like flint, and I know I will not be put to shame."

- The prophetic depiction of the suffering servant reflects Jesus' unwavering obedience despite suffering.

Perfection Through Suffering

Made Perfect

The concept of Jesus being made perfect through suffering means that His experience completed His qualification as the high priest and the source of salvation.

1. Hebrews 2:10: "In bringing many sons and daughters to glory, it was fitting that God, for whom and through whom everything exists, should make the pioneer of their salvation perfect through what he suffered."

- Jesus' suffering perfected Him as the pioneer of salvation, enabling Him to lead many to glory.

2. Hebrews 7:28: "For the law appoints as high priests men in all their weakness; but the oath, which came after the law, appointed the Son, who has been made perfect forever."

- Jesus' perfection as the high priest contrasts with the weaknesses of human high priests appointed under the law.

Expository Study and Strong's Concordance Analysis

Hebrews 5:8 - "Son though he was, he learned obedience from what he suffered."

- Learned (ἔμαθεν, emathen): This verb means to learn or to come to know. Jesus' learning of obedience involves experiential knowledge gained through suffering.

- Strong's Concordance: G3129 – manthanō; to learn, to understand.

- Obedience (ὑπακοήν, hypakoēn): This term refers to compliance or submission. Jesus' obedience was demonstrated through His willing submission to God's will.

- Strong's Concordance: G5218 – hypakoē; obedience, compliance, submission.

- Suffered (ἔπαθεν, epathen): This verb means to suffer or to experience pain. Jesus' suffering was integral to His learning obedience.

- Strong's Concordance: G3958 – paschō; to suffer, to endure.

Hebrews 5:9 - "And, once made perfect, he became the source of eternal salvation for all who obey him."

- Made Perfect (τελειωθείς, teleiōtheis): This verb means to complete or to make perfect. Jesus' perfection was accomplished through His experiences of suffering and obedience.

- Strong's Concordance: G5048 — teleioō; to complete, to make perfect, to finish.

- Source (αἴτιος, aitios): This term refers to the cause or origin. Jesus is the source of eternal salvation because of His perfected obedience.

- Strong's Concordance: G159 — aitios; cause, author, source.

- Eternal (αἰωνίου, aiōniou): This term means everlasting or without end. Jesus' salvation is eternal, emphasizing its enduring nature.

- Strong's Concordance: G166 — aiōnios; eternal, everlasting.

- Obey (ὑπακούουσιν, hypakouousin): This verb means to listen attentively or to submit. Believers are called to obey Jesus as the source of their salvation.

- Strong's Concordance: G5219 — hypakouō; to obey, to submit.

Theological Significance of Learned Obedience

Perfecting Through Suffering

Jesus' obedience and suffering were necessary for His perfection and qualification as the high priest and savior.

1. Romans 5:19: "For just as through the disobedience of the one man the many were made sinners, so also through

the obedience of the one man the many will be made righteous."

- Jesus' obedience contrasts with Adam's disobedience, bringing righteousness and salvation to many.

Source of Eternal Salvation

Jesus' perfection through suffering established Him as the eternal source of salvation for all who obey Him.

1. John 17:2: "For you granted him authority over all people that he might give eternal life to all those you have given him."

- Jesus, granted authority by the Father, provides eternal life to those who follow Him.

2. 1 Peter 1:8-9: "Though you have not seen him, you love him; and even though you do not see him now, you believe in him and are filled with an inexpressible and glorious joy, for you are receiving the end result of your faith, the salvation of your souls."

- Believers' faith in Jesus leads to the salvation of their souls, affirming Jesus as the source of salvation.

Practical Implications for Believers

1. Embracing Suffering: Understanding that Jesus learned obedience through suffering encourages believers to embrace their own sufferings as opportunities for growth and obedience.

2. Obedience to Christ: Believers are called to obey Jesus, recognizing that their obedience is part of the process of receiving eternal salvation.

3. Confidence in Salvation: Knowing that Jesus is the source of eternal salvation provides believers with confidence and assurance in their faith.

4. Living as Christ's Followers: Believers are inspired to live as followers of Christ, imitating His obedience and trust in God, even in the face of suffering.

Conclusion

Hebrews 5:7-10 presents a profound insight into Jesus' learned obedience through suffering, emphasizing His perfection and role as the source of eternal salvation. By exploring these themes through an expository study and analysis using Strong's Concordance, we gain a deeper understanding of the significance of Jesus' obedience and its implications for believers. This understanding enriches our theological knowledge and enhances our faith, guiding us in our relationship with God and our daily walk with Christ.

In the chapters that follow, we will continue to delve into the rich theological insights of Hebrews, drawing lessons that illuminate the significance of Jesus' dual nature and teachings for our lives today.

CHAPTER 06

PERSEVERANCE IN FAITH

Anchor for the Soul: Hope in Christ is Described as an Anchor for the Soul, Firm and Secure, Entering the Inner Sanctuary Behind the Curtain

Key Verses: Hebrews 6:19-20

"We have this hope as an anchor for the soul, firm and secure. It enters the inner sanctuary behind the curtain, where our forerunner, Jesus, has entered on our behalf. He has become a high priest forever, in the order of Melchizedek." (Hebrews 6:19-20, NIV)

Introduction

The book of Hebrews emphasizes the importance of hope in Christ as a steadfast anchor for the soul. This chapter explores the significance of this hope, how it anchors believers in their faith, and its implications for spiritual perseverance. By examining biblical references and employing an expository study with exhaustive Strong's Concordance, we can gain a deeper understanding of the assurance and stability that hope in Christ provides.

Hope in Christ as an Anchor

The Nature of Hope

Hope in Christ is described as an anchor, providing stability and security for the believer's soul.

1. Romans 8:24-25: "For in this hope we were saved. But hope that is seen is no hope at all. Who hopes for what they already have? But if we hope for what we do not yet have, we wait for it patiently."

- Biblical hope is characterized by patient waiting and trust in God's promises, even when they are not yet visible.

2. 1 Peter 1:3-4: "Praise be to the God and Father of our Lord Jesus Christ! In his great mercy he has given us new birth into a living hope through the resurrection of Jesus Christ from the dead, and into an inheritance that can never

perish, spoil or fade. This inheritance is kept in heaven for you."

- Hope is grounded in the resurrection of Jesus and the promise of an eternal inheritance, offering believers a secure future.

The Anchor for the Soul

Hebrews 6:19 describes hope as an anchor, firm and secure, symbolizing stability and reliability.

1. Colossians 1:23: "If you continue in your faith, established and firm, and do not move from the hope held out in the gospel. This is the gospel that you heard and that has been proclaimed to every creature under heaven, and of which I, Paul, have become a servant."

- The gospel provides a firm foundation for hope, encouraging believers to remain steadfast in their faith.

2. Ephesians 4:14: "Then we will no longer be infants, tossed back and forth by the waves, and blown here and there by every wind of teaching and by the cunning and craftiness of people in their deceitful scheming."

- Hope in Christ anchors believers, preventing them from being swayed by false teachings and the uncertainties of life.

Entering the Inner Sanctuary

The Role of Jesus as Forerunner

Jesus, our forerunner, has entered the inner sanctuary behind the curtain, signifying His role as our high priest and mediator.

1. Hebrews 9:24: "For Christ did not enter a sanctuary made with human hands that was only a copy of the true one; he entered heaven itself, now to appear for us in God's presence."

- Jesus' entry into the heavenly sanctuary represents His role in mediating on behalf of believers before God.

2. Hebrews 4:14-16: "Therefore, since we have a great high priest who has ascended into heaven, Jesus the Son of God, let us hold firmly to the faith we profess. For we do not have a high priest who is unable to feel sympathy for our weaknesses, but we have one who has been tempted in every way, just as we are—yet he did not sin. Let us then approach God's throne of grace with confidence, so that we may receive mercy and find grace to help us in our time of need."

- Jesus' priesthood provides believers with the confidence to approach God's throne of grace, knowing that He intercedes for them.

The Inner Sanctuary Behind the Curtain

The inner sanctuary, or the Holy of Holies, was the most sacred place in the Jewish temple, symbolizing God's immediate presence.

1. Leviticus 16:2: "The Lord said to Moses: 'Tell your brother Aaron that he is not to come whenever he chooses into the Most Holy Place behind the curtain in front of the atonement cover on the ark, or else he will die. For I will appear in the cloud over the atonement cover.'"

- The Holy of Holies was accessible only once a year by the high priest, signifying the separation between God and humanity due to sin.

2. Matthew 27:50-51: "And when Jesus had cried out again in a loud voice, he gave up his spirit. At that moment the curtain of the temple was torn in two from top to bottom. The earth shook, the rocks split."

- Jesus' death tore the curtain, symbolizing the removal of the barrier between God and humanity and granting believers direct access to God.

Expository Study and Strong's Concordance Analysis

Hebrews 6:19 - "We have this hope as an anchor for the soul, firm and secure. It enters the inner sanctuary behind the curtain."

- Hope (ἐλπίδα, elpida): This term refers to a confident expectation or trust in God's promises.

- Strong's Concordance: G1680 – elpis; expectation, hope, trust.

- Anchor (ἄγκυραν, ankyran): This term signifies stability and security, likening hope to an anchor that keeps the soul steady.

- Strong's Concordance: G45 – ankura; an anchor.

- Soul (ψυχῆς, psychēs): This term refers to the inner self or life force, representing the whole being of a person.

- Strong's Concordance: G5590 – psychē; soul, life, self.

- Inner Sanctuary (ἐσώτερον τοῦ καταπετάσματος, esōteron tou katapetasmatos): This phrase refers to the innermost part of the temple, the Holy of Holies.

- Strong's Concordance: G2082 – esōteros; inner, inward.

- Strong's Concordance: G2665 – katapetasma; a curtain, veil.

Hebrews 6:20 - "Where our forerunner, Jesus, has entered on our behalf. He has become a high priest forever, in the order of Melchizedek."

- Forerunner (πρόδρομος, prodromos): This term refers to one who goes before, preparing the way for others.

- Strong's Concordance: G4274 – prodromos; a forerunner, precursor.

- High Priest (ἀρχιερεύς, archiereus): This term signifies the chief priest, representing Jesus' role as the ultimate mediator between God and humanity.

- Strong's Concordance: G749 – archiereus; high priest.

- Order (τάξις, taxis): This term refers to arrangement or order, indicating Jesus' unique priesthood in the order of Melchizedek.

- Strong's Concordance: G5010 – taxis; order, arrangement.

Theological Significance of Hope as an Anchor

Stability in Faith

Hope in Christ provides believers with stability, preventing them from being swayed by life's challenges and uncertainties.

1. James 1:6: "But when you ask, you must believe and not doubt, because the one who doubts is like a wave of the sea, blown and tossed by the wind."

- Hope anchors believers, ensuring their faith remains steadfast despite trials.

Confidence in Approach

Believers can confidently approach God's throne, knowing that Jesus has entered the inner sanctuary on their behalf.

1. Ephesians 3:12: "In him and through faith in him we may approach God with freedom and confidence."

- The assurance of Jesus' intercession enables believers to approach God with confidence and boldness.

Practical Implications for Believers

1. Steadfast Hope: Believers are encouraged to hold firmly to their hope in Christ, recognizing it as a secure anchor for their souls.

2. Confident Prayer: Understanding that Jesus intercedes for them, believers can approach God's throne of grace with confidence, seeking mercy and help in times of need.

3. Perseverance in Faith: The imagery of an anchor encourages believers to persevere in their faith, remaining grounded in the promises of God despite challenges.

4. Living with Assurance: The assurance of hope in Christ provides believers with a sense of security and purpose, motivating them to live faithfully and expectantly.

Conclusion

Hebrews 6:19-20 presents a profound insight into the nature of hope in Christ, describing it as an anchor for the soul, firm and secure. By exploring these themes through an expository study and analysis using Strong's Concordance, we gain a deeper understanding of the stability and assurance that hope in Christ provides. This understanding enriches our theological knowledge and enhances our faith, guiding us in our relationship with God and our daily walk with Christ.

In the chapters that follow, we will continue to delve into the rich theological insights of Hebrews, drawing lessons that illuminate the significance of Jesus' dual nature and teachings for our lives today.

FORERUNNER

Jesus, as Our Forerunner, Has Entered on Our Behalf, Having Become a High Priest Forever in the Order of Melchizedek

Key Verses: Hebrews 6:19-20

"We have this hope as an anchor for the soul, firm and secure. It enters the inner sanctuary behind the curtain, where our forerunner, Jesus, has entered on our behalf. He has become a high priest forever, in the order of Melchizedek." (Hebrews 6:19-20, NIV)

Introduction

The book of Hebrews presents Jesus as the forerunner who has entered the heavenly sanctuary on behalf of believers. This chapter explores the significance of Jesus' role as the forerunner, emphasizing His eternal high priesthood in the order of Melchizedek. By examining biblical references and employing an expository study with exhaustive Strong's

Concordance, we can gain a deeper understanding of the assurance and hope that Jesus provides as our forerunner.

Jesus as the Forerunner

Definition and Role of a Forerunner

A forerunner is someone who goes ahead to prepare the way for others, ensuring their safe passage and signaling what is to come.

1. Isaiah 40:3: "A voice of one calling: 'In the wilderness prepare the way for the Lord; make straight in the desert a highway for our God.'"

- This prophetic verse describes the role of a forerunner in preparing the way for the Lord, fulfilled in the ministry of John the Baptist and ultimately in Jesus.

2. John 14:2-3: "My Father's house has many rooms; if that were not so, would I have told you that I am going there to prepare a place for you? And if I go and prepare a place for you, I will come back and take you to be with me that you also may be where I am."

- Jesus assures His disciples that He is going ahead to prepare a place for them, acting as their forerunner.

Jesus Entering on Our Behalf

Hebrews 6:19-20 highlights that Jesus, as our forerunner, has entered the inner sanctuary on our behalf.

1. Hebrews 9:24: "For Christ did not enter a sanctuary made with human hands that was only a copy of the true one; he entered heaven itself, now to appear for us in God's presence."

- Jesus' entry into the heavenly sanctuary signifies His role in representing believers before God, securing their access to His presence.

2. Hebrews 4:14-16: "Therefore, since we have a great high priest who has ascended into heaven, Jesus the Son of God, let us hold firmly to the faith we profess. For we do not have a high priest who is unable to feel sympathy for our weaknesses, but we have one who has been tempted in every way, just as we are—yet he did not sin. Let us then approach God's throne of grace with confidence, so that we may receive mercy and find grace to help us in our time of need."

- Jesus' role as high priest and forerunner provides believers with the confidence to approach God's throne of grace.

High Priest Forever in the Order of Melchizedek

The Order of Melchizedek

Melchizedek is a unique figure in the Old Testament who serves as both king and priest, prefiguring the eternal priesthood of Jesus.

1. Genesis 14:18-20: "Then Melchizedek king of Salem brought out bread and wine. He was priest of God Most High, and he blessed Abram, saying, 'Blessed be Abram by God Most High, Creator of heaven and earth. And praise be to God Most High, who delivered your enemies into your hand.' Then Abram gave him a tenth of everything."

- Melchizedek's dual role as king and priest points to the greater priesthood of Jesus.

2. Psalm 110:4: "The Lord has sworn and will not change his mind: 'You are a priest forever, in the order of Melchizedek.'"

- This messianic psalm predicts an eternal priesthood in the order of Melchizedek, fulfilled in Jesus.

Jesus' Eternal Priesthood

Jesus' priesthood is eternal and superior to the Aaronic priesthood, offering a perfect and unending mediation.

1. Hebrews 7:17-24: "For it is declared: 'You are a priest forever, in the order of Melchizedek.' The former regulation is set aside because it was weak and useless (for the law made nothing perfect), and a better hope is introduced, by which we draw near to God. And it was not without an oath! Others became priests without any oath, but he became a priest with an oath when God said to him: 'The Lord has

sworn and will not change his mind: "You are a priest forever."' Because of this oath, Jesus has become the guarantor of a better covenant. Now there have been many of those priests, since death prevented them from continuing in office; but because Jesus lives forever, he has a permanent priesthood."

- Jesus' eternal priesthood guarantees a better covenant and continuous intercession for believers.

Expository Study and Strong's Concordance Analysis

Hebrews 6:20 - "Where our forerunner, Jesus, has entered on our behalf. He has become a high priest forever, in the order of Melchizedek."

- Forerunner (πρόδρομος, prodromos): This term refers to one who goes before, preparing the way for others.

- Strong's Concordance: G4274 – prodromos; a forerunner, precursor.

- Entered (εἰσῆλθεν, eisēlthen): This verb means to go into or enter, emphasizing Jesus' entry into the heavenly sanctuary.

- Strong's Concordance: G1525 – eiserchomai; to enter, to go into.

- High Priest (ἀρχιερεύς, archiereus): This term signifies the chief priest, representing Jesus' role as the ultimate mediator between God and humanity.

- Strong's Concordance: G749 — archiereus; high priest.

- Order (τάξις, taxis): This term refers to arrangement or order, indicating Jesus' unique priesthood in the order of Melchizedek.

- Strong's Concordance: G5010 — taxis; order, arrangement.

Theological Significance of Jesus as the Forerunner

Assurance of Access

Jesus' role as the forerunner provides believers with the assurance of access to God's presence, as He has already entered on their behalf.

1. Ephesians 2:18: "For through him we both have access to the Father by one Spirit."

- Believers have direct access to the Father through Jesus, facilitated by the Holy Spirit.

2. Romans 5:2: "Through whom we have gained access by faith into this grace in which we now stand. And we boast in the hope of the glory of God."

- Jesus' mediation allows believers to stand in grace and hope for the glory of God.

Eternal Intercession

Jesus' eternal priesthood ensures continuous intercession for believers, providing them with perpetual support and advocacy.

1. 1 John 2:1: "My dear children, I write this to you so that you will not sin. But if anybody does sin, we have an advocate with the Father—Jesus Christ, the Righteous One."

- Jesus advocates for believers before the Father, ensuring their ongoing relationship with God despite their sins.

Practical Implications for Believers

1. Confidence in Salvation: Believers can have complete confidence in their salvation, knowing that Jesus, their forerunner, has entered the heavenly sanctuary on their behalf and continually intercedes for them.

2. Assurance of Access to God: Understanding that Jesus has paved the way, believers are encouraged to approach God's throne of grace with boldness and assurance.

3. Steadfast Faith: The imagery of Jesus as the forerunner encourages believers to remain steadfast in their faith, trusting in the security and hope provided by His eternal priesthood.

4. Living in the New Covenant: Embracing the new covenant mediated by Jesus, believers are called to live in the

fullness of its promises, experiencing a deeper and more intimate relationship with God.

Conclusion

Hebrews 6:19-20 presents a profound insight into Jesus' role as the forerunner, emphasizing His entry into the heavenly sanctuary and His eternal priesthood in the order of Melchizedek. By exploring these themes through an expository study and analysis using Strong's Concordance, we gain a deeper understanding of the assurance and hope that Jesus provides. This understanding enriches our theological knowledge and enhances our faith, guiding us in our relationship with God and our daily walk with Christ.

In the chapters that follow, we will continue to delve into the rich theological insights of Hebrews, drawing lessons that illuminate the significance of Jesus' dual nature and teachings for our lives today.

CHAPTER 07

THE ETERNAL PRIESTHOOD OF MELCHIZEDEK

Superior Priesthood: Jesus' Priesthood, in the Order of Melchizedek, is Superior and Eternal, Unlike the Levitical Priests Who Were Many and Temporary

Key Verses: Hebrews 7:23-28

"Now there have been many of those priests, since death prevented them from continuing in office; but because Jesus lives forever, he has a permanent priesthood. Therefore he is able to save completely those who come to God through him, because he always lives to intercede for them. Such a high priest truly meets our need—one who is holy, blameless, pure, set apart from sinners, exalted above the heavens. Unlike the other high priests, he does not need to offer sacrifices day after day, first for his own sins, and then for the sins of the people. He sacrificed for their sins once for all when he offered himself. For the law appoints as high priests men in all their weakness; but the oath, which came after the law, appointed the Son, who has been made perfect forever." (Hebrews 7:23-28, NIV)

Introduction

The book of Hebrews presents Jesus' priesthood in the order of Melchizedek as superior and eternal, contrasting it with the temporary and numerous Levitical priests. This chapter explores the theological significance of Jesus' superior priesthood, examining biblical references and employing an expository study with exhaustive Strong's Concordance. Understanding Jesus' unique and eternal role enhances our appreciation of His work and its implications for believers.

The Levitical Priesthood

Temporary and Numerous Priests.

The Levitical priests were many because their priesthood was temporary, ending with their deaths.

1. Exodus 28:1: "Have Aaron your brother brought to you from among the Israelites, along with his sons Nadab and Abihu, Eleazar and Ithamar, so they may serve me as priests."

- The priesthood was established through Aaron and his descendants, indicating a hereditary and temporary system.

2. Numbers 20:28: "Moses removed Aaron's garments and put them on his son Eleazar. And Aaron died there on top of the mountain. Then Moses and Eleazar came down from the mountain."

- The death of Aaron and the succession of Eleazar highlight the impermanence of the Levitical priesthood.

Imperfect Sacrifices

The Levitical priests offered sacrifices repeatedly, first for their own sins and then for the people's sins.

1. Leviticus 16:6: "Aaron is to offer the bull for his own sin offering to make atonement for himself and his household."

- The high priest had to offer sacrifices for his own sins, demonstrating his imperfection.

2. Hebrews 10:1-4: "The law is only a shadow of the good things that are coming—not the realities themselves. For this reason it can never, by the same sacrifices repeated endlessly year after year, make perfect those who draw near to worship. Otherwise, would they not have stopped being offered? For the worshipers would have been cleansed once for all, and would no longer have felt guilty for their sins. But

those sacrifices are an annual reminder of sins. It is impossible for the blood of bulls and goats to take away sins."

- The repeated sacrifices of the Levitical system could not achieve permanent purification from sins.

Jesus' Superior and Eternal Priesthood

In the Order of Melchizedek

Jesus' priesthood is in the order of Melchizedek, which is superior and eternal.

1. Genesis 14:18-20: "Then Melchizedek king of Salem brought out bread and wine. He was the priest of God Most High, and he blessed Abram, saying, 'Blessed be Abram by God Most High, Creator of heaven and earth. And praise be to God Most High, who delivered your enemies into your hand.' Then Abram gave him a tenth of everything."

- Melchizedek's unique role as king and priest prefigures Jesus' superior priesthood.

2. Psalm 110:4: "The Lord has sworn and will not change his mind: 'You are a priest forever, in the order of Melchizedek.'"

- This messianic psalm establishes the eternal and unchangeable nature of Jesus' priesthood.

Permanent and Effective Intercession

Jesus' priesthood is permanent and His intercession is effective, offering complete salvation.

1. Hebrews 7:24-25: "But because Jesus lives forever, he has a permanent priesthood. Therefore he is able to save completely those who come to God through him, because he always lives to intercede for them."

- Jesus' eternal life guarantees His continuous and effective intercession for believers.

2. Romans 8:34: "Who then is the one who condemns? No one. Christ Jesus who died—more than that, who was raised to life—is at the right hand of God and is also interceding for us."

- Jesus' intercession at the right hand of God assures believers of their complete salvation.

Once-for-All Sacrifice

Unlike the Levitical priests, Jesus offered Himself once for all, achieving perfect atonement.

1. Hebrews 9:26-28: "Otherwise Christ would have had to suffer many times since the creation of the world. But he has appeared once for all at the culmination of the ages to do away with sin by the sacrifice of himself. Just as people are destined to die once, and after that to face judgment, so Christ was sacrificed once to take away the sins of many; and he will appear a second time, not to bear sin, but to bring salvation to those who are waiting for him."

- Jesus' single sacrifice contrasts with the repeated sacrifices of the Levitical priests, providing definitive atonement.

2. Hebrews 10:10: "And by that will, we have been made holy through the sacrifice of the body of Jesus Christ once for all."

- Believers are made holy through Jesus' once-for-all sacrifice.

Expository Study and Strong's Concordance Analysis

Hebrews 7:24 - "But because Jesus lives forever, he has a permanent priesthood."

- Lives (μένει, menei): This verb means to remain or continue. Jesus' eternal life ensures the permanence of His priesthood.

- Strong's Concordance: G3306 – menō; to remain, abide, continue.

- Permanent (ἀπαράβατον, aparabaton): This term means unchangeable or indestructible. Jesus' priesthood is unending and unalterable.

- Strong's Concordance: G531 – aparabatos; unchangeable, indestructible.

Hebrews 7:25 - "Therefore he is able to save completely those who come to God through him, because he always lives to intercede for them."

- Save (σῴζειν, sōzein): This verb means to save or deliver. Jesus' salvation is comprehensive and complete.

- Strong's Concordance: G4982 – sōzō; to save, deliver, preserve.

- Intercede (ἐντυγχάνειν, entynchanein): This verb means to make intercession or plead. Jesus continually intercedes for believers.

- Strong's Concordance: G1793 – entynchano; to intercede, plead.

Theological Significance of Jesus' Superior Priesthood

Eternal and Perfect Mediation

Jesus' eternal priesthood provides perfect mediation between God and humanity.

1. 1 Timothy 2:5: "For there is one God and one mediator between God and mankind, the man Christ Jesus."

- Jesus' unique role as mediator underscores the perfection and exclusivity of His priesthood.

Complete Salvation

Jesus' superior priesthood ensures complete and eternal salvation for believers.

1. John 10:28-29: "I give them eternal life, and they shall never perish; no one will snatch them out of my hand. My Father, who has given them to me, is greater than all; no one can snatch them out of my Father's hand."

\- Believers' salvation is secure in Jesus' hands, guaranteed by His eternal priesthood.

Practical Implications for Believers

1. Confidence in Salvation: Believers can have unwavering confidence in their salvation, knowing that Jesus' eternal priesthood guarantees their complete redemption.

2. Approaching God with Assurance: Understanding Jesus' continuous intercession encourages believers to approach God with boldness and assurance, knowing they have a perfect mediator.

3. Living in Holiness: Recognizing the efficacy of Jesus' once-for-all sacrifice motivates believers to live in holiness and gratitude for the complete atonement provided.

4. Perseverance in Faith: The permanence and superiority of Jesus' priesthood inspire believers to persevere in their faith, trusting in His eternal intercession and perfect mediation.

Conclusion

Hebrews 7:23-28 presents a profound insight into the superiority and eternality of Jesus' priesthood in the order of Melchizedek. By exploring these themes through an expository study and analysis using Strong's Concordance, we gain a deeper understanding of the unique and perfect nature of Jesus' priesthood and its implications for believers. This understanding enriches our theological knowledge and enhances our faith, guiding us in our relationship with God and our daily walk with Christ.

In the chapters that follow, we will continue to delve into the rich theological insights of Hebrews, drawing lessons that illuminate the significance of Jesus' dual nature and teachings for our lives today.

PERFECT SACRIFICE

Jesus Offered Himself Once for All, a Perfect and Sufficient Sacrifice, Able to Save Completely Those Who Come to God Through Him

Key Verses: Hebrews 7:23-28

"Now there have been many of those priests, since death prevented them from continuing in office; but because Jesus lives forever, he has a permanent priesthood. Therefore he is able to save completely those who come to God through him, because he always lives to intercede for them. Such a high priest truly meets our need—one who is holy, blameless, pure, set apart from sinners, exalted above the heavens. Unlike the other high priests, he does not need to offer sacrifices day after day, first for his own sins, and then for the sins of the people. He sacrificed for their sins once for all when he offered himself. For the law appoints as high priests men in all their weakness; but the oath, which came after the

law, appointed the Son, who has been made perfect forever."
(Hebrews 7:23-28, NIV)

Introduction

The book of Hebrews presents Jesus as the perfect and ultimate high priest who offered Himself as a once-for-all sacrifice. This chapter explores the significance of Jesus' perfect sacrifice, its sufficiency, and its ability to save completely those who come to God through Him. By examining biblical references and employing an expository study with exhaustive Strong's Concordance, we can gain a deeper understanding of the theological implications of Jesus' perfect sacrifice.

The Insufficiency of Levitical Sacrifices

Repeated and Imperfect Sacrifices

The Levitical priests offered sacrifices repeatedly, indicating their insufficiency to provide permanent atonement.

1. Hebrews 10:1-4: "The law is only a shadow of the good things that are coming—not the realities themselves. For this reason, it can never, by the same sacrifices repeated endlessly year after year, make perfect those who draw near to worship. Otherwise, would they not have stopped being offered? For the worshipers would have been cleansed once for all, and would no longer have felt guilty for their sins. But

those sacrifices are an annual reminder of sins. It is impossible for the blood of bulls and goats to take away sins."

- The repetitive nature of Levitical sacrifices highlights their inability to permanently remove sin.

2. Leviticus 16:34: "This is to be a lasting ordinance for you: Atonement is to be made once a year for all the sins of the Israelites."

- The annual Day of Atonement underscores the temporary and repetitive nature of the Levitical sacrifices.

Jesus' Perfect and Sufficient Sacrifice

Once-for-All Sacrifice

Jesus' sacrifice was offered once for all, providing a perfect and sufficient atonement for sin.

1. Hebrews 9:26-28: "Otherwise Christ would have had to suffer many times since the creation of the world. But he has appeared once for all at the culmination of the ages to do away with sin by the sacrifice of himself. Just as people are destined to die once, and after that to face judgment, so Christ was sacrificed once to take away the sins of many; and he will appear a second time, not to bear sin, but to bring salvation to those who are waiting for him."

- Jesus' single sacrifice contrasts with the repeated sacrifices of the Levitical priests, providing definitive atonement.

2. Hebrews 10:10: "And by that will, we have been made holy through the sacrifice of the body of Jesus Christ once for all."

- Believers are made holy through Jesus' once-for-all sacrifice.

Perfect High Priest

Jesus, as the perfect high priest, offered Himself as the perfect sacrifice, fulfilling and surpassing the requirements of the old covenant.

1. Hebrews 7:26-27: "Such a high priest truly meets our need—one who is holy, blameless, pure, set apart from sinners, exalted above the heavens. Unlike the other high priests, he does not need to offer sacrifices day after day, first for his own sins, and then for the sins of the people. He sacrificed for their sins once for all when he offered himself."

- Jesus' holiness and purity qualify Him as the perfect high priest who offered Himself as the perfect sacrifice.

2. 1 Peter 1:18-19: "For you know that it was not with perishable things such as silver or gold that you were redeemed from the empty way of life handed down to you from your ancestors, but with the precious blood of Christ, a lamb without blemish or defect."

- Jesus is described as a lamb without blemish, highlighting the perfection of His sacrifice.

Expository Study and Strong's Concordance Analysis

Hebrews 7:27 - "Unlike the other high priests, he does not need to offer sacrifices day after day, first for his own sins, and then for the sins of the people. He sacrificed for their sins once for all when he offered himself."

- Sacrifices (θυσίας, thysias): This term refers to offerings or sacrifices, indicating the repeated rituals of the Levitical priests.

- Strong's Concordance: G2378 – thysia; a sacrifice, offering.

- Once for All (ἐφάπαξ, ephapax): This term means once and for all or decisively, emphasizing the finality and sufficiency of Jesus' sacrifice.

- Strong's Concordance: G2178 – ephapax; once for all, decisively.

- Offered (προσενέγκας, prosenenkas): This verb means to bring or offer, referring to Jesus' self-sacrifice.

- Strong's Concordance: G4374 – prospherō; to bring, to offer.

Hebrews 9:28 - "So Christ was sacrificed once to take away the sins of many; and he will appear a second time, not to bear sin, but to bring salvation to those who are waiting for him."

- Sacrificed (προσενεχθέντος, prosenechthentos): This verb means to offer or sacrifice, indicating Jesus' offering of Himself.

- Strong's Concordance: G4374 – prospherō; to bring, to offer.

- Take Away (ἀνενεγκεῖν, anenengkein): This verb means to bear or remove, indicating the removal of sins through Jesus' sacrifice.

- Strong's Concordance: G399 – anapherō; to bear, to carry, to remove.

Theological Significance of Jesus' Perfect Sacrifice

Complete and Eternal Salvation

Jesus' perfect sacrifice provides complete and eternal salvation for those who come to God through Him.

1. Hebrews 7:25: "Therefore he is able to save completely those who come to God through him, because he always lives to intercede for them."

- Jesus' continuous intercession ensures the completeness of believers' salvation.

2. John 19:30: "When he had received the drink, Jesus said, 'It is finished.' With that, he bowed his head and gave up his spirit."

- Jesus' declaration of "It is finished" signifies the completion and sufficiency of His sacrificial work.

Fulfillment of the Old Covenant

Jesus' sacrifice fulfills and surpasses the requirements of the old covenant, establishing a new and better covenant.

1. Hebrews 8:6: "But in fact the ministry Jesus has received is as superior to theirs as the covenant of which he is mediator is superior to the old one, since the new covenant is established on better promises."

- The new covenant, mediated by Jesus, is superior and based on better promises, fulfilled through His perfect sacrifice.

Practical Implications for Believers

1. Assurance of Salvation: Believers can have full assurance of their salvation, knowing that Jesus' perfect sacrifice is sufficient and complete.

2. Holiness and Purity: Understanding the perfection of Jesus' sacrifice motivates believers to live in holiness and purity, reflecting the sanctification achieved through His offering.

3. Gratitude and Worship: Recognizing the once-for-all nature of Jesus' sacrifice inspires believers to live in continual gratitude and worship, honoring the immense price paid for their redemption.

4. Perseverance in Faith: The finality and sufficiency of Jesus' sacrifice encourage believers to persevere in their faith, trusting in the complete atonement He has provided.

Conclusion

Hebrews 7:23-28 presents a profound insight into the perfect and sufficient sacrifice of Jesus, emphasizing its once-for-all nature and its ability to save completely those who come to God through Him. By exploring these themes through an expository study and analysis using Strong's Concordance, we gain a deeper understanding of the theological implications of Jesus' perfect sacrifice and its significance for believers. This understanding enriches our theological knowledge and enhances our faith, guiding us in our relationship with God and our daily walk with Christ.

In the chapters that follow, we will continue to delve into the rich theological insights of Hebrews, drawing lessons that illuminate the significance of Jesus' dual nature and teachings for our lives today.

CHAPTER 08

<hr>

THE NEW COVENANT

Mediator of a Better Covenant: Jesus is the Mediator of a New Covenant, Established on Better Promises, Rendering the Old Covenant Obsolete

Key Verses: Hebrews 8:6-13

"But in fact the ministry Jesus has received is as superior to theirs as the covenant of which he is mediator is superior to the old one, since the new covenant is established on better promises. For if there had been nothing wrong with that first covenant, no place would have been sought for another. But God found fault with the people and said: 'The days are coming, declares the Lord, when I will make a new covenant with the people of Israel and with the people of Judah. It will not be like the covenant I made with their ancestors when I took them by the hand to lead them out of Egypt, because they did not remain faithful to my covenant, and I turned away from them, declares the Lord. This is the covenant I will establish with the people of Israel after that time, declares the Lord. I will put my laws in their minds and write them on their hearts. I will be their God, and they will be my people. No longer will they teach their neighbor, or say to one another, 'Know the Lord,' because they will all know me, from the least of them to the greatest. For I will forgive their wickedness and will remember their sins no more.' By calling this covenant 'new,' he has made the first one obsolete; and what is obsolete and outdated will soon disappear." (Hebrews 8:6-13, NIV)

Introduction

The book of Hebrews presents Jesus as the mediator of a new and superior covenant, established on better promises and rendering the old covenant obsolete. This chapter explores the theological significance of the new covenant, its promises, and how it supersedes the old covenant. By examining biblical references and employing an expository study with exhaustive Strong's Concordance, we can gain a deeper understanding of the transformative power of the new covenant mediated by Jesus.

The Old Covenant

The First Covenant and Its Limitations

The old covenant, established through Moses, was based on the law and required continuous sacrifices.

1. Exodus 19:5-6: "Now if you obey me fully and keep my covenant, then out of all nations you will be my treasured possession. Although the whole earth is mine, you will be for me a kingdom of priests and a holy nation."

- The old covenant was conditional upon Israel's obedience to God's laws.

2. Exodus 24:8: "Moses then took the blood, sprinkled it on the people and said, 'This is the blood of the covenant that the Lord has made with you in accordance with all these words.'"

- The old covenant was ratified with the blood of animal sacrifices.

Faults and Weaknesses

The old covenant was limited in its ability to bring about true and lasting transformation.

1. Hebrews 8:7-8: "For if there had been nothing wrong with that first covenant, no place would have been sought for another. But God found fault with the people and

said: 'The days are coming, declares the Lord, when I will make a new covenant with the people of Israel and with the people of Judah.'"

- The first covenant had faults, primarily due to the people's inability to keep it.

2. Galatians 3:19: "Why, then, was the law given at all? It was added because of transgressions until the Seed to whom the promise referred had come. The law was given through angels and entrusted to a mediator."

- The law served as a temporary measure until the coming of Christ, highlighting human transgressions.

The New Covenant Mediated by Jesus

Establishment on Better Promises

The new covenant is established on better promises, focusing on internal transformation and a direct relationship with God.

1. Jeremiah 31:31-34: "'The days are coming,' declares the Lord, 'when I will make a new covenant with the people of Israel and with the people of Judah. It will not be like the covenant I made with their ancestors when I took them by the hand to lead them out of Egypt, because they broke my covenant, though I was a husband to them,' declares the Lord. 'This is the covenant I will make with the people of Israel after that time,' declares the Lord. 'I will put my law in their minds

and write it on their hearts. I will be their God, and they will be my people. No longer will they teach their neighbor, or say to one another, 'Know the Lord,' because they will all know me, from the least of them to the greatest,' declares the Lord. 'For I will forgive their wickedness and will remember their sins no more.'"

- The new covenant promises internal change, personal knowledge of God, and complete forgiveness of sins.

2. 2 Corinthians 3:6: "He has made us competent as ministers of a new covenant—not of the letter but of the Spirit; for the letter kills, but the Spirit gives life."

- The new covenant is of the Spirit, bringing life rather than death through the letter of the law.

Mediator of the New Covenant

Jesus is the mediator of the new covenant, ensuring its efficacy and fulfillment.

1. Hebrews 9:15: "For this reason Christ is the mediator of a new covenant, that those who are called may receive the promised eternal inheritance—now that he has died as a ransom to set them free from the sins committed under the first covenant."

- Jesus' death serves as the ransom that establishes the new covenant, freeing believers from the penalties of the old covenant.

2. 1 Timothy 2:5: "For there is one God and one mediator between God and mankind, the man Christ Jesus."

- Jesus' unique role as mediator bridges the gap between God and humanity.

Expository Study and Strong's Concordance Analysis

Hebrews 8:6 - "But in fact the ministry Jesus has received is as superior to theirs as the covenant of which he is mediator is superior to the old one, since the new covenant is established on better promises."

- Mediator (μεσίτης, mesitēs): This term refers to an intermediary or mediator who facilitates a covenant between two parties.

- Strong's Concordance: G3316 – mesitēs; mediator, intermediary.

- Covenant (διαθήκης, diathēkēs): This term signifies a covenant or agreement, often referring to the divine covenants between God and humanity.

- Strong's Concordance: G1242 – diathēkē; covenant, testament.

- Promises (ἐπαγγελίαις, epangeliais): This term refers to promises, particularly divine promises that assure the fulfillment of God's will.

- Strong's Concordance: G1860 – epangelia; promise, assurance.

Hebrews 8:13 - "By calling this covenant 'new,' he has made the first one obsolete; and what is obsolete and outdated will soon disappear."

- Obsolete (πεπαλαίωκεν, pepalaiōken): This term means to make old or obsolete, indicating the replacement of the old covenant with the new.

- Strong's Concordance: G3822 – palaioō; to make obsolete, to grow old.

- Disappear (ἀφανισμοῦ, aphanismou): This term means to vanish or disappear, signifying the complete fading away of the old covenant.

- Strong's Concordance: G854 – aphanismos; disappearance, vanishing.

Theological Significance of the New Covenant

Internal Transformation

The new covenant emphasizes internal transformation through the indwelling of God's law in the hearts and minds of believers.

1. Ezekiel 36:26-27: "I will give you a new heart and put a new spirit in you; I will remove from you your heart of stone and give you a heart of flesh. And I will put my Spirit in you and move you to follow my decrees and be careful to keep my laws."

- The new covenant involves a spiritual renewal and empowerment to follow God's decrees.

Direct Relationship with God

The new covenant establishes a direct and personal relationship between God and believers, eliminating the need for external mediation.

1. John 14:16-17: "And I will ask the Father, and he will give you another advocate to help you and be with you forever—the Spirit of truth. The world cannot accept him, because it neither sees him nor knows him. But you know him, for he lives with you and will be in you."

- The Holy Spirit, given under the new covenant, facilitates an intimate relationship with God.

Practical Implications for Believers

1. Assurance of Forgiveness: Believers can rest in the assurance of complete forgiveness of sins, knowing that the new covenant promises total and permanent forgiveness.

2. Empowerment by the Spirit: Living under the new covenant means being empowered by the Holy Spirit to live a life pleasing to God, with His laws written on their hearts.

3. Personal Relationship with God: Believers are encouraged to cultivate a direct and personal relationship with God, experiencing His presence and guidance in their daily lives.

4. Living Out the New Covenant: Understanding the superiority of the new covenant motivates believers to live in the fullness of its promises, reflecting the internal transformation and new life it offers.

Conclusion

Hebrews 8:6-13 presents a profound insight into the superiority of the new covenant mediated by Jesus, established on better promises and rendering the old covenant obsolete. By exploring these themes through an expository study and analysis using Strong's Concordance, we gain a deeper understanding of the transformative power of the new covenant and its significance for believers. This understanding enriches our theological knowledge and enhances our faith, guiding us in our relationship with God and our daily walk with Christ.

In the chapters that follow, we will continue to delve into the rich theological insights of Hebrews, drawing lessons

that illuminate the significance of Jesus' dual nature and teachings for our lives today.

INTERNAL LAW

The New Covenant Involves God's Laws Being Written on Believers' Hearts and Minds, and Their Sins Being Remembered No More

Key Verses: Hebrews 8:6-13

"But in fact the ministry Jesus has received is as superior to theirs as the covenant of which he is mediator is superior to the old one, since the new covenant is established on better promises. For if there had been nothing wrong with that first covenant, no place would have been sought for another. But God found fault with the people and said: 'The days are coming, declares the Lord, when I will make a new covenant with the people of Israel and with the people of Judah. It will not be like the covenant I made with their ancestors when I took them by the hand to lead them out of Egypt, because they did not remain faithful to my covenant, and I turned away from them, declares the Lord. This is the covenant I will establish with the people of Israel after that time, declares the Lord. I will put my laws in their minds and write them on their hearts. I will be their God, and they will be my people. No longer will they teach their neighbor, or say to one another, 'Know the Lord,' because they will all know me, from the least of them to the greatest. For I will forgive their wickedness and will remember their sins no more.' By calling this covenant 'new,' he has made the first one obsolete; and what is obsolete and outdated will soon disappear." (Hebrews 8:6-13, NIV)

Introduction

The new covenant, as described in the book of Hebrews, introduces a transformative relationship between God and believers, characterized by God's laws being written on their hearts and minds and their sins being remembered no more. This chapter explores the significance of the internalization of God's law under the new covenant and its implications for believers. By examining biblical references and employing an expository study with exhaustive Strong's Concordance, we can gain a deeper understanding of the new covenant's transformative power.

The Old Covenant and Its External Law

The External Nature of the Old Covenant

The old covenant was characterized by laws written on tablets of stone, requiring external adherence.

1. Exodus 24:12: "The Lord said to Moses, 'Come up to me on the mountain and stay here, and I will give you the tablets of stone with the law and commandments I have written for their instruction.'"

- The old covenant laws were given externally on tablets of stone, emphasizing external obedience.

2. Deuteronomy 4:13: "He declared to you his covenant, the Ten Commandments, which he commanded you to follow and then wrote them on two stone tablets."

- The Ten Commandments, central to the old covenant, were written on stone tablets, symbolizing external regulations.

Limitations of the Old Covenant

The external nature of the old covenant was limited in its ability to bring about true heart transformation.

1. Jeremiah 7:23-24: "But I gave them this command: Obey me, and I will be your God and you will be my people. Walk in obedience to all I command you, that it may go well with you. But they did not listen or pay attention; instead, they followed the stubborn inclinations of their evil hearts. They went backward and not forward."

- The people's inability to obey the external laws revealed the limitations of the old covenant in addressing the heart's condition.

2. Ezekiel 36:26-27: "I will give you a new heart and put a new spirit in you; I will remove from you your heart of stone and give you a heart of flesh. And I will put my Spirit in

you and move you to follow my decrees and be careful to keep my laws."

- The promise of a new heart and spirit under the new covenant addresses the internal transformation needed.

The New Covenant and Its Internal Law

Writing God's Law on Hearts and Minds

The new covenant involves God's laws being internalized, and written on believers' hearts and minds.

1. Jeremiah 31:33: "This is the covenant I will make with the people of Israel after that time," declares the Lord. "I will put my law in their minds and write it on their hearts. I will be their God, and they will be my people."

- The internalization of God's law signifies a profound transformation where obedience flows from within.

2. Romans 2:15: "They show that the requirements of the law are written on their hearts, their consciences also bearing witness, and their thoughts sometimes accusing them and at other times even defending them."

- The new covenant brings about a conscience-led adherence to God's laws, written on the hearts of believers.

Transformation and Relationship

The internalization of God's law fosters a deeper relationship between God and believers, characterized by intimate knowledge and forgiveness.

1. Ezekiel 11:19-20: "I will give them an undivided heart and put a new spirit in them; I will remove from them their heart of stone and give them a heart of flesh. Then they will follow my decrees and be careful to keep my laws. They will be my people, and I will be their God."

- The new covenant promises an undivided heart and a new spirit, enabling a genuine relationship with God.

2. Hebrews 8:12: "For I will forgive their wickedness and will remember their sins no more."

- The new covenant assures complete forgiveness and the removal of sins, enabling a restored relationship with God.

Expository Study and Strong's Concordance Analysis

Hebrews 8:10 - "This is the covenant I will establish with the people of Israel after that time, declares the Lord. I will put my laws in their minds and write them on their hearts. I will be their God, and they will be my people."

- Laws (νόμους, nomous): This term refers to divine laws or principles given by God.

- Strong's Concordance: G3551 – nomos; law, principle.

- Minds (διανοίας, dianoias): This term means the mind, understanding, or intellect.

- Strong's Concordance: G1271 – dianoia; mind, understanding, intellect.

- Hearts (καρδίαις, kardiais): This term refers to the heart, the center of physical and spiritual life.

- Strong's Concordance: G2588 – kardia; heart, inner self.

Hebrews 8:12 - "For I will forgive their wickedness and will remember their sins no more."

- Forgive (ἵλεως, hileōs): This term means to be merciful or forgiving.

- Strong's Concordance: G2436 – hileōs; merciful, forgiving.

- Remember (μνησθήσομαι, mnēsthēsomai): This term means to remember or recall.

- Strong's Concordance: G3415 – mnaomai; to remember, recall.

Theological Significance of the Internal Law

Heart Transformation

The internalization of God's law under the new covenant signifies a fundamental transformation of the believer's heart and mind.

1. 2 Corinthians 3:3: "You show that you are a letter from Christ, the result of our ministry, written not with ink

but with the Spirit of the living God, not on tablets of stone but on tablets of human hearts."

- Believers become living letters of Christ, with God's law written on their hearts by the Spirit.

Personal Relationship with God

The internal law fosters a personal and intimate relationship with God, characterized by direct knowledge and communion.

1. John 14:23: "Jesus replied, 'Anyone who loves me will obey my teaching. My Father will love them, and we will come to them and make our home with them.'"

- The internal law enables believers to experience God's indwelling presence and love.

Practical Implications for Believers

1. Living Out the Law: Believers are called to live out God's law from within, allowing the internal transformation to manifest in their daily lives.

2. Assurance of Forgiveness: The new covenant assures believers of complete forgiveness, enabling them to live in freedom from guilt and shame.

3. Intimate Relationship with God: Believers are encouraged to cultivate an intimate relationship with God, knowing Him personally and experiencing His presence in their lives.

4. Empowered by the Spirit: The internal law is written by the Holy Spirit, empowering believers to follow God's decrees and live in accordance with His will.

Conclusion

Hebrews 8:6-13 presents a profound insight into the internalization of God's law under the new covenant, emphasizing the transformation of hearts and minds and the assurance of complete forgiveness. By exploring these themes through an expository study and analysis using Strong's Concordance, we gain a deeper understanding of the theological implications of the new covenant and its significance for believers. This understanding enriches our theological knowledge and enhances our faith, guiding us in our relationship with God and our daily walk with Christ.

In the chapters that follow, we will continue to delve into the rich theological insights of Hebrews, drawing lessons that illuminate the significance of Jesus' dual nature and teachings for our lives today.

CHAPTER 09

THE PERFECT TABERNACLE AND SACRIFICE

Greater Tabernacle: Christ Entered the Greater and More Perfect Tabernacle Not Made with Human Hands, Signifying His Heavenly Ministry

Key Verses: Hebrews 9:11-14

"But when Christ came as high priest of the good things that are now already here, he went through the greater and more perfect tabernacle that is not made with human hands, that is to say, is not a part of this creation. He did not enter by means of the blood of goats and calves; but he entered the Most Holy Place once for all by his own blood, thus obtaining eternal redemption. The blood of goats and bulls and the ashes of a heifer sprinkled on those who are ceremonially unclean sanctify them so that they are outwardly clean. How much more, then, will the blood of Christ, who through the eternal Spirit offered himself unblemished to God, cleanse our consciences from acts that lead to death, so that we may serve the living God!" (Hebrews 9:11-14, NIV)

Introduction

The book of Hebrews presents Christ as the high priest who entered the greater and more perfect tabernacle, not made with human hands, signifying His heavenly ministry. This chapter explores the significance of the greater tabernacle and how it contrasts with the earthly tabernacle. By examining biblical references and employing an expository study with exhaustive Strong's Concordance, we can gain a deeper understanding of the theological implications of Christ's heavenly ministry.

The Earthly Tabernacle

The Construction of the Earthly Tabernacle

The earthly tabernacle was constructed according to the pattern given by God and served as a place of worship and sacrifice.

1. Exodus 25:8-9: "Then have them make a sanctuary for me, and I will dwell among them. Make this tabernacle and all its furnishings exactly like the pattern I will show you."

- The earthly tabernacle was built according to a divine pattern, emphasizing its importance as a place where God would dwell among His people.

2. Exodus 40:34-35: "Then the cloud covered the tent of meeting, and the glory of the Lord filled the tabernacle. Moses could not enter the tent of meeting because the cloud had settled on it, and the glory of the Lord filled the tabernacle."

- The earthly tabernacle was a physical place where God's presence was manifest.

Limitations of the Earthly Tabernacle

The earthly tabernacle had limitations and could not provide a permanent solution for sin.

1. Hebrews 9:9-10: "This is an illustration for the present time, indicating that the gifts and sacrifices being offered were not able to clear the conscience of the worshiper. They are only a matter of food and drink and various ceremonial washings—external regulations applying until the time of the new order."

- The rituals of the earthly tabernacle were temporary and external, unable to cleanse the conscience of the worshiper.

2. Hebrews 10:1: "The law is only a shadow of the good things that are coming—not the realities themselves. For this reason it can never, by the same sacrifices repeated endlessly year after year, make perfect those who draw near to worship."

- The repetitive sacrifices in the earthly tabernacle were a shadow of the true and lasting solution to sin.

The Greater and More Perfect Tabernacle

Christ's Heavenly Ministry

Christ entered the greater and more perfect tabernacle, signifying His heavenly ministry.

1. Hebrews 9:11: "But when Christ came as high priest of the good things that are now already here, he went through the greater and more perfect tabernacle that is not made with human hands, that is to say, is not a part of this creation."

- The greater tabernacle is a heavenly reality, not part of this creation, signifying a superior ministry.

2. Hebrews 9:24: "For Christ did not enter a sanctuary made with human hands that was only a copy of the true one; he entered heaven itself, now to appear for us in God's presence."

- Christ's entrance into heaven itself underscores the reality and superiority of His ministry compared to the earthly tabernacle.

The Perfect Sacrifice

Christ's sacrifice in the greater tabernacle was perfect and sufficient for eternal redemption.

1. Hebrews 9:12: "He did not enter by means of the blood of goats and calves; but he entered the Most Holy Place once for all by his own blood, thus obtaining eternal redemption."

- Christ's sacrifice, unlike the repeated animal sacrifices, was once for all, securing eternal redemption.

2. Hebrews 10:12-14: "But when this priest had offered for all time one sacrifice for sins, he sat down at the right hand of God, and since that time he waits for his enemies to be made his footstool. For by one sacrifice he has made perfect forever those who are being made holy."

- The single, perfect sacrifice of Christ contrasts with the ongoing sacrifices of the earthly tabernacle, providing lasting perfection for believers.

Expository Study and Strong's Concordance Analysis

Hebrews 9:11 - "But when Christ came as high priest of the good things that are now already here, he went through the greater and more perfect tabernacle that is not made with human hands, that is to say, is not a part of this creation."

- Greater (μεγαλυτέρας, megaluteras): This term means greater or more significant, indicating the superiority of the heavenly tabernacle.

- Strong's Concordance: G3187 – megas; great, large.

- Perfect (τελειοτέρας, teleioteras): This term means more perfect or complete, emphasizing the perfection of the heavenly tabernacle.

- Strong's Concordance: G5046 – teleios; perfect, complete.

- Tabernacle (σκηνῆς, skēnēs): This term refers to a tent or tabernacle, representing the place of worship and God's presence.

- Strong's Concordance: G4633 – skēnē; tent, tabernacle.

Hebrews 9:12 - "He did not enter by means of the blood of goats and calves; but he entered the Most Holy Place once for all by his own blood, thus obtaining eternal redemption."

- Blood (αἵματος, haimatos): This term refers to blood, particularly in the context of sacrificial offerings.

- Strong's Concordance: G129 – haima; blood.

- Eternal (αἰωνίαν, aiōnian): This term means eternal or everlasting, indicating the lasting nature of the redemption obtained by Christ.

- Strong's Concordance: G166 – aiōnios; eternal, everlasting.

- Redemption (λύτρωσιν, lytrōsin): This term means redemption or deliverance, signifying the freeing of believers from sin through Christ's sacrifice.

- Strong's Concordance: G3085 – lytrōsis; redemption, deliverance.

Theological Significance of the Greater Tabernacle

Superiority of Christ's Ministry

Christ's ministry in the greater tabernacle signifies the superiority of the new covenant over the old covenant.

1. Hebrews 8:6: "But the ministry Jesus has received is as superior to theirs as the covenant of which he is mediator is superior to the old one since the new covenant is established on better promises."

- The new covenant, mediated by Christ, is established on better promises, highlighting the superiority of His ministry.

Eternal Redemption

Christ's sacrifice in the heavenly tabernacle secures eternal redemption for believers, contrasting with the temporary solutions of the earthly tabernacle.

1. Hebrews 9:15: "For this reason Christ is the mediator of a new covenant, that those who are called may receive the promised eternal inheritance—now that he has died as a ransom to set them free from the sins committed under the first covenant."

- The eternal inheritance promised under the new covenant is secured through Christ's perfect sacrifice.

Practical Implications for Believers

1. Assurance of Salvation: Believers can have full assurance of their salvation, knowing that Christ's sacrifice in the greater Tabernacle is perfect and complete.

2. Confidence in Approach: Understanding the superiority of Christ's heavenly ministry encourages believers to approach God's throne of grace with confidence.

3. Living in Holiness: Recognizing the eternal redemption secured by Christ motivates believers to live in holiness and dedication to God's service.

4. Gratitude and Worship: The perfect and sufficient sacrifice of Christ inspires believers to live in continual gratitude and worship, honoring the immense price paid for their redemption.

Conclusion

Hebrews 9:11-14 presents a profound insight into the greater and more perfect tabernacle entered by Christ, emphasizing His heavenly ministry and the eternal redemption secured by His perfect sacrifice. By exploring these themes through an expository study and analysis using Strong's Concordance, we gain a deeper understanding of the theological implications of Christ's ministry and its significance for believers. This understanding enriches our theological knowledge and enhances our faith, guiding us in our relationship with God and our daily walk with Christ.

In the chapters that follow, we will continue to delve into the rich theological insights of Hebrews, drawing lessons that illuminate the significance of Jesus' dual nature and teachings for our lives today.

BLOOD OF CHRIST

Blood of Christ: Unlike the Blood of Goats and Calves, Christ's Own Blood Secured Eternal Redemption, Cleansing Our Consciences from Acts that Lead to Death

Key Verses: Hebrews 9:11-14

"But when Christ came as high priest of the good things that are now already here, he went through the greater and more perfect tabernacle that is not made with human hands, that is to say, is not a part of this creation. He did not enter by means of the blood of goats and calves; but he entered the Most Holy Place once for all by his own blood, thus obtaining eternal redemption. The blood of goats and bulls and the ashes of a heifer sprinkled on those who are ceremonially unclean sanctify them so that they are outwardly clean. How much more, then, will the blood of Christ, who through the eternal Spirit offered himself unblemished to God, cleanse our consciences from acts that lead to death, so that we may serve the living God!" (Hebrews 9:11-14, NIV)

Introduction

The book of Hebrews presents the blood of Christ as fundamentally superior to the blood of goats and calves used in the Levitical sacrifices. This chapter explores the theological significance of Christ's blood, which secures eternal redemption and cleanses our consciences from acts that lead to death. By examining biblical references and employing an expository study with exhaustive Strong's Concordance, we can gain a deeper understanding of the transformative power of Christ's sacrifice.

The Levitical Sacrifices

The Blood of Goats and Calves

Under the old covenant, the blood of animals was used for ritual purification and atonement.

1. Leviticus 16:15-16: "He shall then slaughter the goat for the sin offering for the people and take its blood behind the curtain and do with it as he did with the bull's blood: He shall sprinkle it on the atonement cover and in front of it. In this way he will make atonement for the Most Holy Place because of the uncleanness and rebellion of the Israelites, whatever their sins have been."

- The blood of goats was used in the Day of Atonement rituals to make atonement for the people.

2. Numbers 19:9: "A man who is clean shall gather up the ashes of the heifer and put them in a ceremonially clean place outside the camp. They are to be kept by the Israelite community for use in the water of cleansing; it is for purification from sin."

- The ashes of a heifer, mixed with water, were used for ceremonial purification.

Limitations of Animal Sacrifices

The sacrifices of the old covenant were limited and could not provide a permanent solution for sin.

1. Hebrews 10:1-4: "The law is only a shadow of the good things that are coming—not the realities themselves. For this reason, it can never, by the same sacrifices repeated endlessly year after year, make perfect those who draw near to worship. Otherwise, would they not have stopped being

offered? For the worshipers would have been cleansed once for all, and would no longer have felt guilty for their sins. But those sacrifices are an annual reminder of sins. It is impossible for the blood of bulls and goats to take away sins."

- The repetitive nature of animal sacrifices highlighted their insufficiency in providing lasting atonement for sins.

The Blood of Christ

Securing Eternal Redemption

Christ's own blood secured eternal redemption, surpassing the temporary purification offered by animal sacrifices.

1. Hebrews 9:12: "He did not enter by means of the blood of goats and calves; but he entered the Most Holy Place once for all by his own blood, thus obtaining eternal redemption."

- Unlike the Levitical high priests, who entered the Most Holy Place with animal blood, Christ entered with His own blood, securing eternal redemption.

2. Hebrews 9:26-28: "Otherwise Christ would have had to suffer many times since the creation of the world. But he has appeared once for all at the culmination of the ages to do away with sin by the sacrifice of himself. Just as people are destined to die once, and after that to face judgment, so Christ

was sacrificed once to take away the sins of many; and he will appear a second time, not to bear sin, but to bring salvation to those who are waiting for him."

- Christ's single, sufficient sacrifice contrasts with the repeated animal sacrifices, providing definitive atonement for sins.

Cleansing the Conscience

The blood of Christ cleanses our consciences from acts that lead to death, enabling us to serve the living God.

1. Hebrews 9:14: "How much more, then, will the blood of Christ, who through the eternal Spirit offered himself unblemished to God, cleanse our consciences from acts that lead to death, so that we may serve the living God!"

- Christ's blood purifies our inner being, not just our outward actions, allowing us to serve God with a clean conscience.

2. 1 Peter 1:18-19: "For you know that it was not with perishable things such as silver or gold that you were redeemed from the empty way of life handed down to you from your ancestors, but with the precious blood of Christ, a lamb without blemish or defect."

- The precious blood of Christ redeems believers from a futile way of life, emphasizing its value and efficacy.

Expository Study and Strong's Concordance Analysis

Hebrews 9:12 - "He did not enter by means of the blood of goats and calves; but he entered the Most Holy Place once for all by his own blood, thus obtaining eternal redemption."

- Blood (αἵματος, haimatos): This term refers to blood, particularly in the context of sacrificial offerings.

- Strong's Concordance: G129 – haima; blood.

- Eternal (αἰωνίαν, aiōnian): This term means eternal or everlasting, indicating the lasting nature of the redemption obtained by Christ.

- Strong's Concordance: G166 – aiōnios; eternal, everlasting.

- Redemption (λύτρωσιν, lytrōsin): This term means redemption or deliverance, signifying the freeing of believers from sin through Christ's sacrifice.

- Strong's Concordance: G3085 – lytrōsis; redemption, deliverance.

Hebrews 9:14 - "How much more, then, will the blood of Christ, who through the eternal Spirit offered himself unblemished to God, cleanse our consciences from acts that lead to death, so that we may serve the living God!"

- Cleanse (καθαριεῖ, kathariei): This verb means to make clean or purify, indicating the purifying power of Christ's blood.

- Strong's Concordance: G2511 – katharizō; to cleanse, purify.

- Consciences (συνειδήσεως, syneidēseōs): This term refers to the conscience, the inner sense of right and wrong.

- Strong's Concordance: G4893 – syneidēsis; conscience.

- Acts that Lead to Death (νεκρῶν ἔργων, nekrōn ergōn): This phrase refers to dead works or acts that lead to spiritual death.

- Strong's Concordance: G3498 – nekros; dead.

- Strong's Concordance: G2041 – ergon; work, deed.

Theological Significance of the Blood of Christ

Complete and Eternal Redemption

Christ's blood secures complete and eternal redemption, providing a once-for-all solution to the problem of sin.

1. Ephesians 1:7: "In him we have redemption through his blood, the forgiveness of sins, in accordance with the riches of God's grace."

- Redemption and forgiveness are obtained through Christ's blood, highlighting its centrality to salvation.

Inner Purification

The blood of Christ not only provides external purification but also cleanses the conscience, transforming the inner being of believers.

1. 1 John 1:7: "But if we walk in the light, as he is in the light, we have fellowship with one another, and the blood of Jesus, his Son, purifies us from all sin."

- The purifying power of Christ's blood enables believers to live in fellowship and holiness.

Practical Implications for Believers

1. Assurance of Salvation: Believers can have full assurance of their salvation, knowing that Christ's blood provides complete and eternal redemption.

2. Clean Conscience: Understanding that Christ's blood cleanses the conscience encourages believers to live with a sense of inner peace and purity.

3. Service to God: Recognizing the transformative power of Christ's blood motivates believers to serve the living God with a pure heart and clear conscience.

4. Living in Holiness: The cleansing power of Christ's blood calls believers to live in holiness, reflecting the sanctification achieved through His sacrifice.

Conclusion

Hebrews 9:11-14 presents a profound insight into the superiority of Christ's blood over the blood of goats and calves, emphasizing its role in securing eternal redemption and cleansing the conscience. By exploring these themes through an expository study and analysis using Strong's Concordance, we gain a deeper understanding of the theological implications of Christ's sacrifice and its significance for believers. This understanding enriches our theological knowledge and enhances our faith, guiding us in our relationship with God and our daily walk with Christ.

In the chapters that follow, we will continue to delve into the rich theological insights of Hebrews, drawing lessons that illuminate the significance of Jesus' dual nature and teachings for our lives today.

CHAPTER 10

THE ONCE-FOR-ALL SACRIFICE

Bold Access: Believers Have Confidence to Enter the Most Holy Place by the Blood of Jesus, Through a New and Living Way Opened for Us

Key Verses: Hebrews 10:19-25

"Therefore, brothers and sisters, since we have confidence to enter the Most Holy Place by the blood of Jesus, by a new and living way opened for us through the curtain, that is, his body, and since we have a great priest over the house of God, let us draw near to God with a sincere heart and with the full assurance that faith brings, having our hearts sprinkled to cleanse us from a guilty conscience and having our bodies washed with pure water. Let us hold unswervingly to the hope we profess, for he who promised is faithful. And let us consider how we may spur one another on toward love and good deeds, not giving up meeting together, as some are in the habit of doing, but encouraging one another—and all the more as you see the Day approaching." (Hebrews 10:19-25, NIV)

Introduction

The book of Hebrews emphasizes the unique privilege believers have in approaching God with confidence, thanks to the once-for-all sacrifice of Jesus Christ. This chapter explores the concept of bold access to the Most Holy Place, made possible through the blood of Jesus, and the implications for believers. By examining biblical references and employing an expository study with exhaustive Strong's Concordance, we can gain a deeper understanding of the significance of this access and its impact on our faith and community life.

The Most Holy Place

The Old Covenant Restrictions

Under the old covenant, access to the Most Holy Place was restricted and only allowed once a year by the high priest.

1. Leviticus 16:2: "The Lord said to Moses: 'Tell your brother Aaron that he is not to come whenever he chooses into the Most Holy Place behind the curtain in front of the atonement cover on the ark, or else he will die. For I will appear in the cloud over the atonement cover.'"

- The high priest could only enter the Most Holy Place on the Day of Atonement, signifying the restricted access to God's presence.

2. Hebrews 9:7: "But only the high priest entered the inner room, and that only once a year, and never without blood, which he offered for himself and for the sins the people had committed in ignorance."

- The annual entrance of the high priest with sacrificial blood highlighted the limited access under the old covenant.

The Curtain as a Barrier

The curtain in the tabernacle and later in the temple served as a physical barrier separating the Most Holy Place from the rest of the sanctuary.

1. Exodus 26:31-33: "Make a curtain of blue, purple and scarlet yarn and finely twisted linen, with cherubim woven into it by a skilled worker. Hang it with gold hooks on four posts of acacia wood overlaid with gold and standing on four silver bases. Hang the curtain from the clasps and place the

ark of the covenant law behind the curtain. The curtain will separate the Holy Place from the Most Holy Place."

- The curtain symbolizes the separation between God and humanity due to sin.

2. Matthew 27:50-51: "And when Jesus had cried out again in a loud voice, he gave up his spirit. At that moment the curtain of the temple was torn in two from top to bottom. The earth shook, the rocks split."

- The tearing of the temple curtain at Jesus' death signifies the removal of the barrier between God and humanity.

Bold Access Through Jesus

Confidence to Enter

Believers now have confidence to enter the Most Holy Place by the blood of Jesus.

1. Hebrews 10:19: "Therefore, brothers and sisters, since we have confidence to enter the Most Holy Place by the blood of Jesus."

- The sacrificial blood of Jesus provides believers with the confidence to approach God's presence boldly.

2. Ephesians 3:12: "In him and through faith in him we may approach God with freedom and confidence."

- Faith in Jesus grants believers the freedom and confidence to approach God.

A New and Living Way

Jesus inaugurated a new and living way through His flesh, granting believers direct access to God.

1. Hebrews 10:20: "By a new and living way opened for us through the curtain, that is, his body."

- Jesus' body, sacrificed on the cross, serves as the new way to access God's presence.

2. John 14:6: "Jesus answered, 'I am the way and the truth and the life. No one comes to the Father except through me.'"

- Jesus Himself is the way to the Father, providing a living path to God.

Expository Study and Strong's Concordance Analysis

Hebrews 10:19 - "Therefore, brothers and sisters, since we have confidence to enter the Most Holy Place by the blood of Jesus."

- Confidence (παρρησίαν, parrēsian): This term means boldness or assurance, indicating the freedom believers have to approach God.

- Strong's Concordance: G3954 – parrēsia; boldness, confidence, openness.

- Blood (αἵματος, haimatos): This term refers to blood, particularly in the context of sacrificial offerings.

- Strong's Concordance: G129 – haima; blood.

- Most Holy Place (τὰ ἅγια, ta hagia): This term refers to the innermost part of the sanctuary, the Holy of Holies.

- Strong's Concordance: G39 – hagios; holy, sacred.

Hebrews 10:20 - "By a new and living way opened for us through the curtain, that is, his body."

- New (πρόσφατον, prosphaton): This term means freshly slaughtered or recently slain, indicating something new and living.

- Strong's Concordance: G4372 – prosphatos; new, freshly slain.

- Living (ζῶσαν, zōsan): This term means living or alive, emphasizing the dynamic nature of the way Jesus opened.

- Strong's Concordance: G2198 – zaō; to live, to be alive.

- Curtain (καταπετάσματος, katapetasmatos): This term refers to the veil or curtain in the temple.

- Strong's Concordance: G2665 – katapetasma; curtain, veil.

Theological Significance of Bold Access

Full Assurance of Faith

Believers are encouraged to draw near to God with a sincere heart and full assurance of faith.

1. Hebrews 10:22: "Let us draw near to God with a sincere heart and with the full assurance that faith brings, having our hearts sprinkled to cleanse us from a guilty conscience and having our bodies washed with pure water."

- The full assurance of faith allows believers to approach God with confidence, knowing they are cleansed and purified.

Holding Unswervingly to Hope

Believers are called to hold firmly to the hope they profess, relying on the faithfulness of God.

1. Hebrews 10:23: "Let us hold unswervingly to the hope we profess, for he who promised is faithful."

- The confidence in God's promises motivates believers to remain steadfast in their hope.

Practical Implications for Believers

1. Confidence in Prayer: Believers can approach God boldly in prayer, knowing that they have access to the Most Holy Place through Jesus' sacrifice.

2. Living in Assurance: The assurance of faith and the purification provided by Jesus' blood enable believers to live with a clear conscience and a confident heart.

3. Encouraging One Another: Understanding the bold access to God encourages believers to gather together, spur

one another on toward love and good deeds, and support each other in their faith journey.

4. Steadfast Hope: Holding firmly to the hope professed in Jesus empowers believers to remain steadfast and unwavering, trusting in the faithfulness of God's promises.

Conclusion

Hebrews 10:19-25 presents a profound insight into the bold access believers have to the Most Holy Place through the blood of Jesus, emphasizing the new and living way He opened for us. By exploring these themes through an expository study and analysis using Strong's Concordance, we gain a deeper understanding of the theological implications of this access and its significance for our faith and community life. This understanding enriches our theological knowledge and enhances our faith, guiding us in our relationship with God and our daily walk with Christ.

In the chapters that follow, we will continue to delve into the rich theological insights of Hebrews, drawing lessons that illuminate the significance of Jesus' dual nature and teachings for our lives today.

ENCOURAGEMENT TO PRESERVER

Encouragement to Persevere: Encouraged to Draw Near to God with a Sincere Heart, Hold Unswervingly to

Hope, and Spur One Another On Towards Love and Good Deeds

Key Verses: Hebrews 10:19-25

"Therefore, brothers and sisters, since we have the confidence to enter the Most Holy Place by the blood of Jesus, by a new and living way opened for us through the curtain, that is, his body, and since we have a great priest over the house of God, let us draw near to God with a sincere heart and with the full assurance that faith brings, having our hearts sprinkled to cleanse us from a guilty conscience and having our bodies washed with pure water. Let us hold unswervingly to the hope we profess, for he who promised is faithful. And let us consider how we may spur one another on toward love and good deeds, not giving up meeting together, as some are in the habit of doing, but encouraging one another—and all the more as you see the Day approaching." (Hebrews 10:19-25, NIV)

Introduction

The book of Hebrews provides profound encouragement for believers to persevere in their faith. This chapter explores the exhortation to draw near to God with a sincere heart, hold unswervingly to hope, and spur one another on towards love and good deeds. By examining biblical references and employing an expository study with exhaustive Strong's Concordance, we can gain a deeper understanding of the importance of perseverance and mutual encouragement in the Christian life.

Drawing Near to God

A Sincere Heart and Full Assurance

Believers are encouraged to draw near to God with sincerity and full assurance of faith, made possible through Christ's sacrifice.

1. Hebrews 10:22: "Let us draw near to God with a sincere heart and with the full assurance that faith brings, having our hearts sprinkled to cleanse us from a guilty conscience and having our bodies washed with pure water."

- The call to draw near to God emphasizes a genuine approach, free from guilt, made possible by Christ's cleansing sacrifice.

2. James 4:8: "Come near to God and he will come near to you. Wash your hands, you sinners, and purify your hearts, you double-minded."

- Drawing near to God involves a commitment to purity and sincerity, leading to a closer relationship with Him.

Cleansed Conscience

The blood of Jesus purifies believers from a guilty conscience, enabling them to approach God confidently.

1. Hebrews 9:14: "How much more, then, will the blood of Christ, who through the eternal Spirit offered himself unblemished to God, cleanse our consciences from acts that lead to death, so that we may serve the living God!"

- Christ's sacrifice cleanses the conscience, freeing believers from the burden of guilt and enabling them to serve God wholeheartedly.

2. 1 John 1:9: "If we confess our sins, he is faithful and just and will forgive us our sins and purify us from all unrighteousness."

- The promise of forgiveness and purification through confession and faith in Christ's sacrifice assures believers of their cleansed state before God.

Holding Unswervingly to Hope

The Faithfulness of God

Believers are called to hold firmly to the hope they profess, grounded in the faithfulness of God.

1. Hebrews 10:23: "Let us hold unswervingly to the hope we profess, for he who promised is faithful."

- The encouragement to hold unswervingly to hope is based on the unwavering faithfulness of God who keeps His promises.

2. Lamentations 3:22-23: "Because of the Lord's great love we are not consumed, for his compassions never fail. They are new every morning; great is your faithfulness."

- God's faithfulness and steadfast love provide a secure foundation for the hope believers hold.

The Hope of Eternal Life

The hope professed by believers is the assurance of eternal life and the fulfillment of God's promises.

1. Titus 1:2: "In the hope of eternal life, which God, who does not lie, promised before the beginning of time."

- The hope of eternal life is a key component of the Christian faith, promised by a God who does not lie.

2. 1 Peter 1:3-4: "Praise be to the God and Father of our Lord Jesus Christ! In his great mercy he has given us new birth into a living hope through the resurrection of Jesus Christ from the dead, and into an inheritance that can never perish, spoil or fade. This inheritance is kept in heaven for you."

- The living hope through the resurrection of Jesus assures believers of an eternal inheritance, reinforcing their perseverance in faith.

Spurring One Another On Towards Love and Good Deeds

Mutual Encouragement

Believers are encouraged to consider how to motivate one another towards love and good deeds, fostering a supportive and active community.

1. Hebrews 10:24: "And let us consider how we may spur one another on toward love and good deeds."

- The call to spur one another on highlights the importance of mutual encouragement and active participation in the faith community.

2. Galatians 6:2: "Carry each other's burdens, and in this way you will fulfill the law of Christ."

- Supporting one another in love and good deeds fulfills the law of Christ, emphasizing communal responsibility.

The Importance of Meeting Together

Regular fellowship and gathering are essential for mutual encouragement and spiritual growth.

1. Hebrews 10:25: "Not giving up meeting together, as some are in the habit of doing, but encouraging one another—and all the more as you see the Day approaching."

- The exhortation to not forsake meeting together underscores the importance of communal worship and encouragement, especially in anticipation of Christ's return.

2. Acts 2:42: "They devoted themselves to the apostles' teaching and to fellowship, to the breaking of bread and to prayer."

- The early church's devotion to fellowship and communal activities serves as a model for believers to follow.

Expository Study and Strong's Concordance Analysis

Hebrews 10:22 - "Let us draw near to God with a sincere heart and with the full assurance that faith brings, having our hearts sprinkled to cleanse us from a guilty conscience and having our bodies washed with pure water."

- Draw Near (προσερχώμεθα, proserchōmetha): This term means to approach or come near, emphasizing the act of approaching God.

- Strong's Concordance: G4334 – proserchomai; to approach, draw near.

- Sincere Heart (ἀληθινῆς καρδίας, alēthinēs kardias): This phrase means a true or genuine heart, indicating sincerity and authenticity.

- Strong's Concordance: G228 – alēthinos; true, genuine.

- Strong's Concordance: G2588 – kardia; heart, inner self.

- Full Assurance (πληροφορία, plērophoria): This term means full assurance or complete certainty, indicating strong confidence in faith.

- Strong's Concordance: G4136 – plērophoria; full assurance, certainty.

Hebrews 10:23 - "Let us hold unswervingly to the hope we profess, for he who promised is faithful."

- Hold Unswervingly (κατέχωμεν, katechōmen): This term means to hold fast or firmly, indicating steadfastness.

- Strong's Concordance: G2722 – katechō; to hold fast, retain.

- Hope (ἐλπίδος, elpidos): This term means hope or expectation, indicating the confident expectation of future good.

- Strong's Concordance: G1680 – elpis; hope, expectation.

Hebrews 10:24 - "And let us consider how we may spur one another on toward love and good deeds."

- Consider (κατανοῶμεν, katanoōmen): This term means to consider or contemplate, indicating careful thought.

- Strong's Concordance: G2657 – katanoeō; to consider, perceive.

- Spur On (παροξυσμὸν, paroxysmon): This term means to provoke or stimulate, indicating motivation.

- Strong's Concordance: G3948 – paroxysmos; provocation, stimulation.

Theological Significance of Encouragement to Persevere

The Role of Community in Perseverance

Mutual encouragement and communal support are essential for believers to persevere in their faith.

1. 1 Thessalonians 5:11: "Therefore encourage one another and build each other up, just as in fact you are doing."

- Building each other up through encouragement strengthens the faith community.

The Assurance of God's Faithfulness

God's faithfulness provides the foundation for believers to hold unswervingly to their hope.

1. 2 Timothy 2:13: "If we are faithless, he remains faithful, for he cannot disown himself."

- God's unchanging faithfulness assures believers of His promises, motivating perseverance.

Practical Implications for Believers

1. Drawing Near to God: Believers are encouraged to approach God confidently and sincerely, embracing the cleansing and assurance provided by Christ's sacrifice.

2. Holding Firm to Hope: Believers should hold firmly to their hope in Christ, grounded in the faithfulness of God, and remain steadfast in their faith.

3. Spurring One Another: On Believers are called to actively encourage one another towards love and good deeds, fostering a supportive and motivating community.

4. Regular Fellowship: Regular gathering and fellowship with other believers are crucial for mutual encouragement and spiritual growth, especially as they anticipate Christ's return.

Conclusion

Hebrews 10:19-25 presents a profound exhortation for believers to persevere in their faith by drawing near to God with a sincere heart, holding unswervingly to hope, and spurring one another on towards love and good deeds. By exploring these themes through an expository study and analysis using Strong's Concordance, we gain a deeper understanding of the importance of perseverance and mutual encouragement in the Christian life. This understanding enriches our theological knowledge and enhances our faith, guiding us in our relationship with God and our daily walk with Christ.

In the chapters that follow, we will continue to delve into the rich theological insights of Hebrews, drawing lessons

that illuminate the significance of Jesus' dual nature and teachings for our lives today.

CHAPTER 11

FAITH IN ACTION

Definition of Faith: Faith is Confidence in What We Hope For and Assurance About What We Do Not See

Key Verses: Hebrews 11:1-6

"Now faith is confidence in what we hope for and assurance about what we do not see. This is what the ancients were commended for. By faith, we understand that the universe was formed at God's command so that what is seen was not made out of what was visible. By faith, Abel brought God a better offering than Cain did. By faith, he was commended as righteous, when God spoke well of his offerings. And by faith Abel still speaks, even though he is dead. By faith Enoch was taken from this life, so that he did not experience death: 'He could not be found, because God had taken him away.' For before he was taken, he was commended as one who pleased God. And without faith it is impossible to please God, because anyone who comes to him must believe that he exists and that he rewards those who earnestly seek him." (Hebrews 11:1-6, NIV)

Introduction

The book of Hebrews provides a comprehensive definition of faith and illustrates it through the lives of biblical figures. This chapter explores the nature of faith as confidence in what we hope for and assurance about what we do not see. By examining biblical references and employing an expository study with exhaustive Strong's Concordance, we can gain a deeper understanding of faith and its significance in the life of a believer.

The Nature of Faith

Confidence in What We Hope For

Faith involves a confident expectation of the fulfillment of God's promises.

1. Hebrews 11:1: "Now faith is confidence in what we hope for and assurance about what we do not see."

- Faith is characterized by a confident trust in the future fulfillment of God's promises.

2. Romans 8:24-25: "For in this hope we were saved. But hope that is seen is no hope at all. Who hopes for what they already have? But if we hope for what we do not yet have, we wait for it patiently."

- Faith involves a confident expectation of things not yet seen, grounded in the hope of salvation.

Assurance About What We Do Not See

Faith provides assurance and conviction regarding realities that are not visible to the human eye.

1. 2 Corinthians 5:7: "For we live by faith, not by sight."

- Faith transcends physical sight, offering assurance of unseen spiritual realities.

2. Hebrews 11:3: "By faith we understand that the universe was formed at God's command, so that what is seen was not made out of what was visible."

- Faith provides understanding and conviction about the invisible work of God in creation.

Expository Study and Strong's Concordance Analysis

Hebrews 11:1 - "Now faith is confidence in what we hope for and assurance about what we do not see."

- Faith (πίστις, pistis): This term refers to trust, belief, or confidence in God and His promises.

- Strong's Concordance: G4102 – pistis; faith, belief, trust.

- Confidence (ὑπόστασις, hypostasis): This term means assurance, confidence, or substance, indicating the foundational nature of faith.

- Strong's Concordance: G5287 – hypostasis; confidence, substance, assurance.

- Assurance (ἔλεγχος, elegchos): This term means conviction or evidence, indicating the certainty faith provides about unseen realities.

- Strong's Concordance: G1650 – elegchos; conviction, evidence.

Faith in the Lives of the Ancients

Abel's Faith

Abel's faith was demonstrated through his offering, which was commended by God as righteous.

1. Hebrews 11:4: "By faith Abel brought God a better offering than Cain did. By faith he was commended as righteous, when God spoke well of his offerings. And by faith Abel still speaks, even though he is dead."

- Abel's faith led him to offer a pleasing sacrifice to God, demonstrating his righteousness and enduring legacy.

2. Genesis 4:4: "And Abel also brought an offering—fat portions from some of the firstborn of his flock. The Lord looked with favor on Abel and his offering."

- Abel's faith was evident in his choice of offering, which pleased God.

Enoch's Faith

Enoch's faith pleased God, resulting in him being taken away without experiencing death.

1. Hebrews 11:5: "By faith Enoch was taken from this life, so that he did not experience death: 'He could not be found, because God had taken him away.' For before he was taken, he was commended as one who pleased God."

- Enoch's faith led to a unique testimony of pleasing God, culminating in his being taken away without death.

2. Genesis 5:24: "Enoch walked faithfully with God; then he was no more, because God took him away."

- Enoch's faithful walk with God was marked by a close relationship that led to his translation to heaven.

Theological Significance of Faith

Faith and Pleasing God

Faith is essential for pleasing God and receiving His rewards.

1. Hebrews 11:6: "And without faith it is impossible to please God, because anyone who comes to him must believe that he exists and that he rewards those who earnestly seek him."

- Faith is foundational to a relationship with God, as it involves believing in His existence and His responsiveness to those who seek Him.

2. Romans 4:3: "What does Scripture say? 'Abraham believed God, and it was credited to him as righteousness.'"

- Faith is credited as righteousness, as demonstrated in the life of Abraham.

Faith and Understanding

Faith provides understanding and insight into spiritual and unseen realities.

1. Hebrews 11:3: "By faith we understand that the universe was formed at God's command, so that what is seen was not made out of what was visible."

- Faith allows believers to comprehend the divine act of creation, understanding that the visible universe was formed by the invisible word of God.

Practical Implications for Believers

1. Living by Faith: Believers are called to live by faith, trusting in God's promises and the unseen realities of His kingdom.

2. Confidence in God's Promises: Faith provides the confidence and assurance needed to hold onto God's promises, even when they are not immediately visible.

3. Pleasing God: Faith is essential for pleasing God, as it involves trusting in His character and His rewards for those who diligently seek Him.

4. Understanding Spiritual Realities: Faith provides insight into spiritual truths and divine actions, offering a deeper understanding of God's work in the world.

Conclusion

Hebrews 11:1-6 presents a profound definition of faith as confidence in what we hope for and assurance about what we do not see. By exploring these themes through an expository study and analysis using Strong's Concordance, we gain a deeper understanding of the nature of faith and its significance in the life of a believer. This understanding enriches our theological knowledge and enhances our faith, guiding us in our relationship with God and our daily walk with Christ.

In the chapters that follow, we will continue to delve into the rich theological insights of Hebrews, drawing lessons that illuminate the significance of Jesus' dual nature and teachings for our lives today.

HEROES OF FAITH

Heroes of Faith: The Chapter Lists Numerous Examples of Faith from Old Testament Saints, Culminating in the Ultimate Example of Jesus

Key Verses: Hebrews 11:1-40

"Now faith is confidence in what we hope for and assurance about what we do not see. This is what the ancients were commended for... And what more shall I say? I do not have time to tell about Gideon, Barak, Samson and Jephthah, about David and Samuel and the prophets, who through faith conquered kingdoms, administered justice, and gained what was promised; who shut the mouths of lions, quenched the fury of the flames, and escaped the edge of the sword; whose weakness was turned to strength; and who became powerful in battle and routed foreign armies." (Hebrews 11:1-2, 32-34, NIV)

Introduction

Hebrews 11, often referred to as the "Faith Hall of Fame," provides a comprehensive list of Old Testament heroes whose lives exemplified faith. This chapter explores the lives and faith of these individuals, culminating in the ultimate example of faith in Jesus Christ. By examining biblical references and employing an expository study with exhaustive Strong's Concordance, we gain a deeper understanding of the role of faith in the lives of these heroes and its significance for believers today.

Definition of Faith

Confidence and Assurance

Faith is defined as confidence in what we hope for and assurance about what we do not see.

1. Hebrews 11:1: "Now faith is confidence in what we hope for and assurance about what we do not see."

- Faith involves a confident expectation of God's promises and a conviction of unseen realities.

2. Hebrews 11:6: "And without faith it is impossible to please God, because anyone who comes to him must believe that he exists and that he rewards those who earnestly seek him."

- Faith is essential for pleasing God and involves believing in His existence and His rewards for those who seek Him.

Heroes of Faith

Abel: Faith in Offering

Abel demonstrated faith through his offering, which was accepted by God.

1. Hebrews 11:4: "By faith Abel brought God a better offering than Cain did. By faith he was commended as

righteous, when God spoke well of his offerings. And by faith Abel still speaks, even though he is dead."

- Abel's faith was shown in his sacrifice, which was pleasing to God and serves as a lasting testimony.

2. Genesis 4:4: "And Abel also brought an offering—fat portions from some of the firstborn of his flock. The Lord looked with favor on Abel and his offering."

- Abel's choice of offering demonstrated his faith and righteousness.

Enoch: Faith in Pleasing God

Enoch's faith was demonstrated in his close walk with God, resulting in him being taken away without experiencing death.

1. Hebrews 11:5: "By faith Enoch was taken from this life, so that he did not experience death: 'He could not be found, because God had taken him away.' For before he was taken, he was commended as one who pleased God."

- Enoch's faith led to a unique testimony of pleasing God and being taken directly to heaven.

2. Genesis 5:24: "Enoch walked faithfully with God; then he was no more, because God took him away."

- Enoch's faithfulness and close relationship with God exemplify a life of faith.

Noah: Faith in Obedience

Noah's faith led him to build an ark in obedience to God's command, saving his family from the flood.

1. Hebrews 11:7: "By faith Noah, when warned about things not yet seen, in holy fear built an ark to save his family. By his faith he condemned the world and became heir of the righteousness that is in keeping with faith."

- Noah's faith was shown through his obedience to God's warning and his action in building the ark.

2. Genesis 6:22: "Noah did everything just as God commanded him."

- Noah's complete obedience to God's instructions highlights his faith.

Abraham: Faith in Promise

Abraham's faith was demonstrated in his willingness to leave his homeland and trust in God's promises.

1. Hebrews 11:8-10: "By faith Abraham, when called to go to a place he would later receive as his inheritance, obeyed and went, even though he did not know where he was going. By faith he made his home in the promised land like a stranger in a foreign country; he lived in tents, as did Isaac and Jacob, who were heirs with him of the same promise. For he was looking forward to the city with foundations, whose architect and builder is God."

- Abraham's faith was shown in his willingness to obey God's call and trust in His promises.

2. Genesis 12:1-4: "The Lord had said to Abram, 'Go from your country, your people and your father's household to the land I will show you.' So Abram went, as the Lord had told him."

- Abraham's immediate obedience to God's command demonstrates his faith.

Sarah: Faith in God's Faithfulness

Sarah's faith was shown in her belief in God's promise to give her a son, despite her old age.

1. Hebrews 11:11: "And by faith even Sarah, who was past childbearing age, was enabled to bear children because she considered him faithful who had made the promise."

- Sarah's faith rested on her belief in God's faithfulness to fulfill His promise.

2. Genesis 21:1-2: "Now the Lord was gracious to Sarah as he had said, and the Lord did for Sarah what he had promised. Sarah became pregnant and bore a son to Abraham in his old age, at the very time God had promised him."

- The fulfillment of God's promise to Sarah underscores her faith in His word.

Faith in the Lives of Other Heroes

Isaac, Jacob, and Joseph

Isaac, Jacob, and Joseph demonstrated faith in their blessings and instructions for future generations.

1. Hebrews 11:20-22: "By faith Isaac blessed Jacob and Esau in regard to their future. By faith Jacob, when he was dying, blessed each of Joseph's sons, and worshiped as he leaned on the top of his staff. By faith Joseph, when his end was near, spoke about the exodus of the Israelites from Egypt and gave instructions concerning the burial of his bones."

- These patriarchs showed faith in God's promises and foresaw future events concerning their descendants.

Moses: Faith in Deliverance

Moses' faith was shown in his refusal to be known as the son of Pharaoh's daughter and his choice to suffer with the people of God.

1. Hebrews 11:24-26: "By faith Moses, when he had grown up, refused to be known as the son of Pharaoh's daughter. He chose to be mistreated along with the people of God rather than to enjoy the fleeting pleasures of sin. He regarded disgrace for the sake of Christ as of greater value than the treasures of Egypt, because he was looking ahead to his reward."

- Moses' faith led him to identify with God's people and seek God's reward over earthly treasures.

2. Exodus 2:11-12: "One day, after Moses had grown up, he went out to where his own people were and watched them at their hard labor. He saw an Egyptian beating a Hebrew, one of his own people."

- Moses' actions demonstrate his faith and commitment to God's purposes for his people.

The Ultimate Example of Faith: Jesus

Jesus' Perfect Faith

Jesus is presented as the ultimate example of faith, whose perfect life and sacrificial death provide the foundation for believers' faith.

1. Hebrews 12:2: "Fixing our eyes on Jesus, the pioneer and perfecter of faith. For the joy set before him he endured the cross, scorning its shame, and sat down at the right hand of the throne of God."

- Jesus is the pioneer and perfecter of faith, demonstrating perfect trust and obedience to God.

2. Philippians 2:8: "And being found in appearance as a man, he humbled himself by becoming obedient to death— even death on a cross!"

- Jesus' obedience to God's will, even to the point of death, exemplifies ultimate faith.

Expository Study and Strong's Concordance Analysis

Hebrews 11:1 - "Now faith is confidence in what we hope for and assurance about what we do not see."

- Faith (πίστις, pistis): This term refers to trust, belief, or confidence in God and His promises.

- Strong's Concordance: G4102 – pistis; faith, belief, trust.

- Confidence (ὑπόστασις, hypostasis): This term means assurance, confidence, or substance, indicating the foundational nature of faith.

- Strong's Concordance: G5287 – hypostasis; confidence, substance, assurance.

- Assurance (ἔλεγχος, elegchos): This term means conviction or evidence, indicating the certainty faith provides about unseen realities.

- Strong's Concordance: G1650 – elegchos; conviction, evidence.

Theological Significance of the Heroes of Faith

The Legacy of Faith

The lives of these heroes provide a legacy of faith, demonstrating trust in God's promises and obedience to His commands.

1. Hebrews 11:39-40: "These were all commended for their faith, yet none of them received what had been

promised, since God had planned something better for us so that only together with us would they be made perfect."

- The heroes of faith were commended for their trust in God, even though they did not receive the complete fulfillment of the promises during their lifetimes.

Faith and Righteousness

Faith is credited as righteousness, as seen in the lives of these heroes.

1. Romans 4:3: "What does Scripture say? 'Abraham believed God, and it was credited to him as righteousness.'"

- Abraham's faith was counted as righteousness, exemplifying the principle that faith leads to righteousness.

Practical Implications for Believers

1. Living by Faith: Believers are encouraged to live by faith, following the examples of the heroes of faith who trusted in God's promises and acted in obedience to His commands.

2. Confidence in God's Promises: The stories of the heroes of faith provide assurance and confidence in the reliability of God's promises, motivating believers to hold firmly to their faith.

3. Endurance in Trials: The faith of these heroes, despite challenges and trials, encourages believers to persevere and remain steadfast in their faith journey.

4. Looking to Jesus: Believers are called to fix their eyes on Jesus, the ultimate example of faith, and follow His example of trust and obedience to God.

Conclusion

Hebrews 11 presents a profound list of heroes of faith, highlighting their trust in God and obedience to His commands. By exploring these examples through an expository study and analysis using Strong's Concordance, we gain a deeper understanding of the role of faith in the lives of these heroes and its significance for believers today. This understanding enriches our theological knowledge and enhances our faith, guiding us in our relationship with God and our daily walk with Christ.

In the chapters that follow, we will continue to delve into the rich theological insights of Hebrews, drawing lessons that illuminate the significance of Jesus' dual nature and teachings for our lives today.

CHAPTER 12

THE EXAMPLE OF JESUS

Fixing Eyes on Jesus: Encouraged to Run the Race with Perseverance, Fixing Our Eyes on Jesus, the Pioneer and Perfecter of Faith

Key Verses: Hebrews 12:1-3

"Therefore, since we are surrounded by such a great cloud of witnesses, let us throw off everything that hinders and the sin that so easily entangles. And let us run with perseverance the race marked out for us, fixing our eyes on Jesus, the pioneer and perfecter of faith. For the joy set before him he endured the cross, scorning its shame, and sat down at the right hand of the throne of God. Consider him who endured such opposition from sinners, so that you will not grow weary and lose heart." (Hebrews 12:1-3, NIV)

Introduction

The book of Hebrews encourages believers to run their spiritual race with perseverance, fixing their eyes on Jesus, the pioneer and perfecter of faith. This chapter explores the importance of focusing on Jesus, drawing inspiration from His example to endure hardships and remain steadfast in faith. By examining biblical references and employing an expository study with exhaustive Strong's Concordance, we can gain a deeper understanding of the significance of fixing our eyes on Jesus.

Running the Race with Perseverance

Surrounded by a Great Cloud of Witnesses

Believers are encouraged by the examples of the heroes of faith who have gone before them.

1. Hebrews 12:1: "Therefore, since we are surrounded by such a great cloud of witnesses, let us throw off everything that hinders and the sin that so easily entangles. And let us run with perseverance the race marked out for us."

- The "great cloud of witnesses" refers to the heroes of faith mentioned in Hebrews 11, whose lives of faith inspire believers to persevere.

2. 1 Corinthians 9:24: "Do you not know that in a race all the runners run, but only one gets the prize? Run in such a way as to get the prize."

- Believers are encouraged to run their spiritual race with the determination to win the prize, inspired by those who have finished their race in faith.

Throwing Off Hindrances and Sin

Believers are called to remove anything that hinders their spiritual progress and to avoid sin that entangles them.

1. Hebrews 12:1: "Let us throw off everything that hinders and the sin that so easily entangles."

- Throwing off hindrances and sin is essential for running the race with perseverance.

2. Colossians 3:8: "But now you must also rid yourselves of all such things as these: anger, rage, malice, slander, and filthy language from your lips."

- Believers are instructed to rid themselves of sinful behaviors that can hinder their spiritual growth.

Fixing Our Eyes on Jesus

The Pioneer and Perfecter of Faith

Jesus is described as the pioneer and perfecter of faith, providing the ultimate example for believers.

1. Hebrews 12:2: "Fixing our eyes on Jesus, the pioneer and perfecter of faith."

- Jesus is the pioneer (author) and perfecter (finisher) of faith, serving as the ultimate example for believers to follow.

2. Philippians 1:6: "Being confident of this, that he who began a good work in you will carry it on to completion until the day of Christ Jesus."

- Jesus, who began the work of faith in believers, will also bring it to completion.

Endurance and Joy in Suffering

Jesus endured the cross, motivated by the joy set before Him, providing a model of endurance in suffering.

1. Hebrews 12:2: "For the joy set before him he endured the cross, scorning its shame, and sat down at the right hand of the throne of God."

- Jesus' endurance of the cross, motivated by future joy, serves as an example for believers to endure their own trials.

2. Isaiah 53:11: "After he has suffered, he will see the light of life and be satisfied; by his knowledge, my righteous servant will justify many, and he will bear their iniquities."

- Jesus' suffering was purposeful, leading to satisfaction and the justification of many.

Expository Study and Strong's Concordance Analysis

Hebrews 12:1 - "Therefore, since we are surrounded by such a great cloud of witnesses, let us throw off everything that hinders and the sin that so easily entangles. And let us run with perseverance the race marked out for us."

- Witnesses (μαρτύρων, martyron): This term refers to those who bear witness, testify, or have testified.

- Strong's Concordance: G3144 – martys; witness, one who testifies.

- Perseverance (ὑπομονῆς, hypomonēs): This term means endurance, patience, or steadfastness.

- Strong's Concordance: G5281 – hypomonē; endurance, perseverance, patience.

- Race (ἀγῶνα, agōna): This term refers to a contest, struggle, or race.

- Strong's Concordance: G73 – agōn; a contest, struggle, race.

Hebrews 12:2 - "Fixing our eyes on Jesus, the pioneer and perfecter of faith. For the joy set before him he endured the cross, scorning its shame, and sat down at the right hand of the throne of God."

- Fixing (ἀφορῶντες, aphorōntes): This term means to look away from other things and focus on one object.

- Strong's Concordance: G872 – aphoraō; to look away, to fix one's gaze upon.

- Pioneer (ἀρχηγὸν, archēgon): This term means author, leader, or pioneer.

- Strong's Concordance: G747 – archēgos; author, leader, pioneer.

- Perfecter (τελειωτὴν, teleiōtēn): This term means finisher or one who completes.

- Strong's Concordance: G5051 – teleiōtēs; finisher, perfecter.

Theological Significance of Fixing Eyes on Jesus

Jesus as the Ultimate Example

Jesus, as the pioneer and perfecter of faith, provides the ultimate example for believers to follow in their spiritual journey.

1. 1 Peter 2:21: "To this you were called, because Christ suffered for you, leaving you an example, that you should follow in his steps."

- Jesus' life and suffering serve as a model for believers to emulate.

Motivation and Endurance

Fixing our eyes on Jesus provides motivation and endurance to persevere through trials and challenges.

1. Romans 5:3-5: "Not only so, but we also glory in our sufferings, because we know that suffering produces perseverance; perseverance, character; and character, hope.

And hope does not put us to shame, because God's love has been poured out into our hearts through the Holy Spirit, who has been given to us."

- Endurance in trials leads to spiritual growth and hope, strengthened by focusing on Jesus.

Practical Implications for Believers

1. Focus on Jesus: Believers are encouraged to focus on Jesus, drawing strength and inspiration from His example of faith and endurance.

2. Endurance in Trials: By fixing their eyes on Jesus, believers can endure trials and challenges with perseverance, knowing that Jesus has gone before them.

3. Running the Race: Believers are called to run their spiritual race with determination, removing any hindrances and sins that could entangle them.

4. Encouragement from Witnesses: The examples of the heroes of faith provide encouragement and motivation for believers to persevere in their own faith journey.

Conclusion

Hebrews 12:1-3 presents a profound exhortation for believers to run their spiritual race with perseverance, fixing their eyes on Jesus, the pioneer and perfecter of faith. By exploring these themes through an expository study and analysis using Strong's Concordance, we gain a deeper understanding of the significance of focusing on Jesus and its impact on our faith and endurance. This understanding enriches our theological knowledge and enhances our faith, guiding us in our relationship with God and our daily walk with Christ.

In the chapters that follow, we will continue to delve into the rich theological insights of Hebrews, drawing lessons that illuminate the significance of Jesus' dual nature and teachings for our lives today.

ENDURANCE OF THE CROSS

Jesus Endured the Cross, Scorning Its Shame, and Is Now Seated at the Right Hand of the Throne of God, an Example for Believers to Consider in Their Own Struggles

Key Verses: Hebrews 12:1-3

"Therefore, since we are surrounded by such a great cloud of witnesses, let us throw off everything that hinders and the sin that so easily entangles. And let us run with perseverance the race marked out for us, fixing our eyes on Jesus, the pioneer and perfecter of faith. For the joy set before him he endured the cross, scorning its shame, and sat down at the right hand of the throne of God. Consider him who endured such opposition from sinners, so that you will not grow weary and lose heart." (Hebrews 12:1-3, NIV)

Introduction

The endurance of Jesus Christ on the cross is a profound example for believers to consider in their own struggles. This chapter explores the significance of Jesus' endurance, His attitude towards the shame of the cross, and His exaltation at the right hand of God. By examining biblical references and employing an expository study with exhaustive Strong's Concordance, we can gain a deeper understanding of how Jesus' endurance serves as a model for believers facing their own trials.

The Endurance of Jesus

The Path to the Cross

Jesus' journey to the cross involved immense physical and emotional suffering, which He endured for the sake of humanity's salvation.

1. Hebrews 12:2: "For the joy set before him he endured the cross, scorning its shame, and sat down at the right hand of the throne of God."

- Jesus endured the cross, motivated by the joy of accomplishing God's redemptive plan.

2. Isaiah 53:3-5: "He was despised and rejected by mankind, a man of suffering, and familiar with pain. Like one from whom people hide their faces he was despised, and we held him in low esteem. Surely he took up our pain and bore our suffering, yet we considered him punished by God,

stricken by him, and afflicted. But he was pierced for our transgressions, he was crushed for our iniquities; the punishment that brought us peace was on him, and by his wounds we are healed."

- Isaiah's prophecy highlights the suffering and endurance of the Messiah, which Jesus fulfilled on the cross.

Scorning Its Shame

Jesus faced the shame and humiliation of the cross with a resolute attitude, focusing on the greater purpose.

1. Hebrews 12:2: "Scorning its shame."

- Jesus disregarded the shame of the cross, understanding its role in God's plan for redemption.

2. Philippians 2:8: "And being found in appearance as a man, he humbled himself by becoming obedient to death—even death on a cross!"

- Jesus' humility and obedience led Him to endure the shameful and painful death on the cross.

Expository Study and Strong's Concordance Analysis

Hebrews 12:2 - "Fixing our eyes on Jesus, the pioneer and perfecter of faith. For the joy set before him he endured the cross, scorning its shame, and sat down at the right hand of the throne of God."

- Endured (ὑπέμεινεν, hypemeinen): This term means to remain, to persevere, or to endure.

- Strong's Concordance: G5278 – hypomenō; to remain, to endure, to persevere.

- Scorning (καταφρονήσας, kataphronēsas): This term means to despise or to think little of.

- Strong's Concordance: G2706 – kataphroneō; to despise, to disdain.

- Shame (αἰσχύνης, aischynēs): This term refers to disgrace or shame.

- Strong's Concordance: G152 – aischynē; shame, disgrace.

- Sat Down (ἐκάθισεν, ekathisen): This term means to sit down or to take a seat, often indicating a position of authority.

- Strong's Concordance: G2523 – kathizō; to sit down, to settle, to take a seat.

Theological Significance of Jesus' Endurance

Motivation by Joy

Jesus was motivated by the joy set before Him, which included the fulfillment of God's plan and the redemption of humanity.

1. Hebrews 12:2: "For the joy set before him."

- The anticipated joy of fulfilling God's will and redeeming humanity motivated Jesus to endure the cross.

2. Isaiah 53:11: "After he has suffered, he will see the light of life and be satisfied; by his knowledge, my righteous servant will justify many, and he will bear their iniquities."

- The satisfaction and joy of accomplishing God's redemptive work were key motivations for Jesus.

Exaltation and Authority

After enduring the cross, Jesus was exalted and seated at the right hand of the throne of God, signifying His authority and completed work.

1. Hebrews 12:2: "And sat down at the right hand of the throne of God."

- Jesus' exaltation to God's right hand signifies His authority and the completion of His redemptive work.

2. Philippians 2:9-11: "Therefore God exalted him to the highest place and gave him the name that is above every name, that at the name of Jesus every knee should bow, in heaven and on earth and under the earth, and every tongue acknowledge that Jesus Christ is Lord, to the glory of God the Father."

- Jesus' exaltation and authority are recognized universally, highlighting His lordship.

Practical Implications for Believers

Enduring Personal Trials

Believers are encouraged to endure their own trials by looking to Jesus' example of endurance.

1. Hebrews 12:3: "Consider him who endured such opposition from sinners, so that you will not grow weary and lose heart."

- Reflecting on Jesus' endurance helps believers to persevere through their own struggles without losing heart.

2. James 1:2-4: "Consider it pure joy, my brothers and sisters, whenever you face trials of many kinds, because you know that the testing of your faith produces perseverance. Let perseverance finish its work so that you may be mature and complete, not lacking anything."

- Trials are opportunities for spiritual growth and maturity, requiring perseverance inspired by Jesus' example.

Scorning Shame

Believers can find strength in Jesus' example to scorn shame and focus on the joy of fulfilling God's purposes.

1. Romans 8:18: "I consider that our present sufferings are not worth comparing with the glory that will be revealed in us."

- The future glory far outweighs present sufferings, encouraging believers to endure with a focus on God's promises.

Perseverance and Focus

Fixing our eyes on Jesus, believers are called to persevere in their faith journey with determination and focus.

1. 1 Corinthians 15:58: "Therefore, my dear brothers and sisters, stand firm. Let nothing move you. Always give yourselves fully to the work of the Lord, because you know that your labor in the Lord is not in vain."

- Believers are encouraged to remain steadfast and fully committed to God's work, inspired by Jesus' endurance.

Conclusion

Hebrews 12:1-3 presents a profound example of Jesus' endurance of the cross, His attitude towards its shame, and His subsequent exaltation. By exploring these themes through an expository study and analysis using Strong's Concordance, we gain a deeper understanding of how Jesus' endurance serves as a model for believers facing their own trials. This understanding enriches our theological knowledge and enhances our faith, guiding us in our relationship with God and our daily walk with Christ.

In the chapters that follow, we will continue to delve into the rich theological insights of Hebrews, drawing lessons that illuminate the significance of Jesus' dual nature and teachings for our lives today.

CHAPTER 13

PRACTICAL EXHORTATIONS AND BENEDICTION

Living Out Faith: Instructions on Loving One Another, Hospitality, Marriage, and Contentment

Key Verses: Hebrews 13:1-8

"Keep on loving one another as brothers and sisters. Do not forget to show hospitality to strangers, for by so doing some people have shown hospitality to angels without knowing it. Continue to remember those in prison as if you were together with them in prison and those who are mistreated as if you yourselves were suffering. Marriage should be honored by all, and the marriage bed kept pure, for God will judge the adulterer and all the sexually immoral. Keep your lives free from the love of money and be content with what you have, because God has said, 'Never will I leave you; never will I forsake you.' So we say with confidence, 'The Lord is my helper; I will not be afraid. What can mere mortals do to me?' Remember your leaders, who spoke the word of God to you. Consider the outcome of their way of life and imitate their faith. Jesus Christ is the same yesterday and today and forever." (Hebrews 13:1-8, NIV)

Introduction

The final chapter of Hebrews provides practical exhortations for living out faith in everyday life. This chapter explores instructions on loving one another, hospitality, marriage, and contentment, offering a guide for believers to embody their faith through actions. By examining biblical references and employing an expository study with exhaustive Strong's Concordance, we gain a deeper understanding of these practical teachings and their significance for believers.

Loving One Another

Brotherly Love

Believers are encouraged to continue loving one another as brothers and sisters in Christ.

1. Hebrews 13:1: "Keep on loving one another as brothers and sisters."

- The call to brotherly love emphasizes the importance of mutual affection and support within the Christian community.

2. John 13:34-35: "A new command I give you: Love one another. As I have loved you, so you must love one another. By this everyone will know that you are my disciples, if you love one another."

- Jesus commands His disciples to love one another, demonstrating their identity as His followers.

Hospitality to Strangers

Believers are instructed to show hospitality to strangers, recognizing the potential for divine encounters.

1. Hebrews 13:2: "Do not forget to show hospitality to strangers, for by so doing some people have shown hospitality to angels without knowing it."

- Hospitality is a significant expression of love, and it can lead to unexpected blessings.

2. Genesis 18:1-5: "The Lord appeared to Abraham near the great trees of Mamre while he was sitting at the entrance to his tent in the heat of the day. Abraham looked up and saw three men standing nearby. When he saw them, he hurried from the entrance of his tent to meet them and

bowed low to the ground. He said, 'If I have found favor in your eyes, my lord, do not pass your servant by. Let a little water be brought, and then you may all wash your feet and rest under this tree. Let me get you something to eat, so you can be refreshed and then go on your way—now that you have come to your servant.' 'Very well,' they answered, 'do as you say.'"

- Abraham's hospitality to strangers, who turned out to be divine visitors, highlights the importance of welcoming others.

Remembering Those in Need

Compassion for Prisoners and the Mistreated

Believers are called to remember those in prison and those who are mistreated, empathizing with their suffering.

1. Hebrews 13:3: "Continue to remember those in prison as if you were together with them in prison and those who are mistreated as if you yourselves were suffering."

- Compassion and solidarity with those in difficult circumstances are essential expressions of Christian love.

2. Matthew 25:36: "I needed clothes and you clothed me, I was sick and you looked after me, I was in prison and you came to visit me."

- Jesus identifies with the needy and emphasizes the importance of caring for those in distress.

Honoring Marriage

Purity and Commitment

Marriage is to be honored by all, and purity within marriage is to be maintained.

1. Hebrews 13:4: "Marriage should be honored by all, and the marriage bed kept pure, for God will judge the adulterer and all the sexually immoral."

- The sanctity of marriage is to be upheld, and faithfulness within marriage is paramount.

2. Ephesians 5:31-33: "For this reason, a man will leave his father and mother and be united to his wife, and the two will become one flesh. This is a profound mystery—but I am talking about Christ and the church. However, each one of you also must love his wife as he loves himself, and the wife must respect her husband."

- Marriage reflects the relationship between Christ and the church, emphasizing mutual love and respect.

Contentment and Trust

Freedom from the Love of Money

Believers are instructed to keep their lives free from the love of money and to be content with what they have.

1. Hebrews 13:5: "Keep your lives free from the love of money and be content with what you have, because God has said, 'Never will I leave you; never will I forsake you.'"

- Contentment and trust in God's provision are crucial for a faithful Christian life.

2. 1 Timothy 6:6-10: "But godliness with contentment is great gain. For we brought nothing into the world, and we can take nothing out of it. But if we have food and clothing, we will be content with that. Those who want to get rich fall into temptation and a trap and into many foolish and harmful desires that plunge people into ruin and destruction. For the love of money is the root of all kinds of evil. Some people, eager for money, have wandered from the faith and pierced themselves with many griefs."

- The love of money leads to many pitfalls, and contentment with God's provision is encouraged.

Expository Study and Strong's Concordance Analysis

Hebrews 13:1 - "Keep on loving one another as brothers and sisters."

- Loving (φιλαδελφία, philadelphia): This term refers to brotherly love or fraternal affection.

- Strong's Concordance: G5360 – philadelphia; brotherly love, affection for fellow believers.

Hebrews 13:2 - "Do not forget to show hospitality to strangers, for by so doing some people have shown hospitality to angels without knowing it."

- Hospitality (φιλοξενίας, philoxenias): This term means the love of strangers or hospitality.

- Strong's Concordance: G5381 – philoxenia; hospitality, love of strangers.

Hebrews 13:5 - "Keep your lives free from the love of money and be content with what you have, because God has said, 'Never will I leave you; never will I forsake you.'"

- Content (ἀρκούμενοι, arkoumenoi): This term means to be satisfied or content.

- Strong's Concordance: G714 – arkeō; to be sufficient, to be content.

- Love of Money (ἀφιλάργυρος, aphilargyros): This term refers to being free from the love of money.

- Strong's Concordance: G866 – aphilargyros; not loving money, free from avarice.

Theological Significance of Living Out Faith

Genuine Christian Community

The practical exhortations in Hebrews 13 emphasize the importance of living out faith through love, hospitality, compassion, and integrity, reflecting a genuine Christian community.

1. Galatians 6:2: "Carry each other's burdens, and in this way you will fulfill the law of Christ."

- Mutual support and burden-sharing are essential components of a vibrant Christian community.

Trust in God's Provision

Contentment and trust in God's provision are central to the Christian life, demonstrating reliance on His faithfulness.

1. Philippians 4:11-13: "I am not saying this because I am in need, for I have learned to be content whatever the circumstances. I know what it is to be in need, and I know what it is to have plenty. I have learned the secret of being content in any and every situation, whether well fed or hungry, whether living in plenty or in want. I can do all this through him who gives me strength."

- Trusting in God's provision allows believers to find contentment in all circumstances.

Practical Implications for Believers

1. Loving One Another: Believers are encouraged to love one another as brothers and sisters, fostering a supportive and affectionate community.

2. Showing Hospitality: Hospitality to strangers is an important expression of Christian love, potentially leading to divine encounters.

3. Honoring Marriage: Upholding the sanctity of marriage and maintaining purity within marriage are essential aspects of living out faith.

4. Contentment and Trust: Believers are called to live free from the love of money, finding contentment in God's provision and trusting in His faithfulness.

Conclusion

Hebrews 13:1-8 provides practical exhortations for living out faith in everyday life, emphasizing love, hospitality, marriage, and contentment. By exploring these instructions through an expository study and analysis using Strong's Concordance, we gain a deeper understanding of how to embody our faith through actions. This understanding enriches our theological knowledge and enhances our faith, guiding us in our relationship with God and our daily walk with Christ.

In the chapters that follow, we will continue to delve into the rich theological insights of Hebrews, drawing lessons that illuminate the significance of Jesus' dual nature and teachings for our lives today.

PRACTICAL EXHORTATIONS AND BENEDICTION

Unchanging Christ: Jesus Christ is the Same Yesterday, Today, and Forever, Providing a Stable Foundation for Faith and Life

Key Verses: Hebrews 13:8

"Jesus Christ is the same yesterday and today and forever." (Hebrews 13:8, NIV)

Introduction

The constancy of Jesus Christ serves as a cornerstone for Christian faith and life. Hebrews 13:8 highlights the unchanging nature of Jesus, emphasizing His eternal consistency and reliability. This chapter explores the theological significance of Jesus' unchanging nature and its implications for believers. By examining biblical references and employing an expository study with exhaustive Strong's Concordance, we gain a deeper understanding of the stability and assurance found in Christ.

The Unchanging Nature of Christ

Consistency in Character and Purpose

Jesus Christ's character and purpose remain constant through all ages.

1. Hebrews 13:8: "Jesus Christ is the same yesterday and today and forever."

   - This verse affirms the eternal constancy of Jesus Christ, underscoring His reliability and faithfulness.

2. James 1:17: "Every good and perfect gift is from above, coming down from the Father of the heavenly lights, who does not change like shifting shadows."

- God's unchanging nature is mirrored in Jesus Christ, providing a foundation for faith and trust.

Eternal Existence

Jesus' eternal existence affirms His unchanging nature.

1. John 1:1-2: "In the beginning was the Word, and the Word was with God, and the Word was God. He was with God in the beginning."

- Jesus, the Word, existed from the beginning, highlighting His eternal nature.

2. Revelation 1:8: "'I am the Alpha and the Omega,' says the Lord God, 'who is, and who was, and who is to come, the Almighty.'"

- Jesus' eternal existence as the Alpha and Omega emphasizes His constancy through all time.

Expository Study and Strong's Concordance Analysis

Hebrews 13:8 - "Jesus Christ is the same yesterday and today and forever."

- Same (ὁ αὐτός, ho autos): This term means the same, identical, or unchanged.

- Strong's Concordance: G846 — autos; self, the same, identical.

- Yesterday (ἐχθές, echthes): This term refers to the day before today, indicating past time.

- Strong's Concordance: G5504 — echthes; yesterday, the day before.

- Today (σήμερον, sēmeron): This term means today, indicating the present time.

- Strong's Concordance: G4594 — sēmeron; today, this day.

- Forever (εἰς τοὺς αἰῶνας, eis tous aiōnas): This term means into the ages, indicating eternity.

- Strong's Concordance: G165 — aiōn; an age, a long period, eternity.

Theological Significance of the Unchanging Christ

Stability and Assurance

The unchanging nature of Jesus Christ provides stability and assurance for believers.

1. Malachi 3:6: "I the Lord do not change. So you, the descendants of Jacob, are not destroyed."

- God's immutability offers stability and assurance, mirrored in the unchanging nature of Jesus.

2. Psalm 102:25-27: "In the beginning, you laid the foundations of the earth, and the heavens are the work of your hands. They will perish, but you remain; they will all wear out like a garment. Like clothing, you will change them and they will be discarded. But you remain the same, and your years will never end."

- God's eternal constancy provides a foundation for trust and security, reflected in Jesus Christ.

Faithfulness in Promises

Jesus' unchanging nature guarantees the fulfillment of His promises.

1. 2 Corinthians 1:20: "For no matter how many promises God has made, they are 'Yes' in Christ. And so through him the 'Amen' is spoken by us to the glory of God."

- The fulfillment of God's promises in Jesus Christ is assured by His unchanging nature.

2. Hebrews 6:17-18: "Because God wanted to make the unchanging nature of his purpose very clear to the heirs of what was promised, he confirmed it with an oath. God did this so that, by two unchangeable things in which it is impossible for God to lie, we who have fled to take hold of the hope set before us may be greatly encouraged."

- God's unchangeable purpose and promises provide encouragement and hope for believers.

Practical Implications for Believers

Trust and Confidence

Believers can place their trust and confidence in Jesus, knowing that He is eternally reliable.

1. Hebrews 13:5-6: "Keep your lives free from the love of money and be content with what you have, because God

has said, 'Never will I leave you; never will I forsake you.' So we say with confidence, 'The Lord is my helper; I will not be afraid. What can mere mortals do to me?'"

- The unchanging presence and help of Jesus encourage believers to trust in Him fully.

Steadfast Faith

The constancy of Jesus inspires believers to remain steadfast in their faith.

1. 1 Corinthians 15:58: "Therefore, my dear brothers and sisters, stand firm. Let nothing move you. Always give yourselves fully to the work of the Lord, because you know that your labor in the Lord is not in vain."

- The assurance of Jesus' unchanging nature motivates believers to stand firm and remain dedicated to God's work.

Consistency in Life and Doctrine

Believers are called to maintain consistency in their lives and doctrines, reflecting the unchanging nature of Christ.

1. Ephesians 4:14-15: "Then we will no longer be infants, tossed back and forth by the waves, and blown here and there by every wind of teaching and by the cunning and craftiness of people in their deceitful scheming. Instead, speaking the truth in love, we will grow to become in every

respect the mature body of him who is the head, that is, Christ."

- Consistency in doctrine and life is essential for spiritual maturity, modeled after the unchanging Christ.

Conclusion

Hebrews 13:8 provides a profound affirmation of the unchanging nature of Jesus Christ, underscoring His eternal constancy and reliability. By exploring these themes through an expository study and analysis using Strong's Concordance, we gain a deeper understanding of the theological significance of Jesus' unchanging nature and its implications for believers. This understanding enriches our theological knowledge and enhances our faith, guiding us in our relationship with God and our daily walk with Christ.

As we conclude this study of Hebrews, we are reminded of the rich theological insights and practical exhortations provided throughout the book, encouraging us to live out our faith with confidence and perseverance, anchored in the unchanging nature of Jesus Christ.

CONCLUSION

The book of Hebrews presents a comprehensive picture of Jesus Christ as divine, eternal, and supreme. This epistle masterfully emphasizes His unique role as the high priest, the perfect sacrifice, and the mediator of a new covenant, providing profound insights into His divinity and teachings. By delving into these lessons, believers can gain a deeper understanding of their faith and draw closer to the One who is the author and perfecter of their salvation.

The Divinity of Jesus Christ

Supreme Revelation

Jesus is the ultimate revelation of God, surpassing all previous prophets and messengers.

1. Hebrews 1:1-3: "In the past God spoke to our ancestors through the prophets at many times and in various ways, but in these last days he has spoken to us by his Son, whom he appointed heir of all things, and through whom also he made the universe. The Son is the radiance of God's glory and the exact representation of his being, sustaining all things by his powerful word."

- Jesus' divinity is affirmed through His role as the final and supreme revelation of God, the heir of all things, and the sustainer of the universe.

Eternal Priesthood

Jesus' priesthood is eternal and superior to the Levitical priesthood, being in the order of Melchizedek.

1. Hebrews 7:24-25: "But because Jesus lives forever, he has a permanent priesthood. Therefore he is able to save completely those who come to God through him, because he always lives to intercede for them."

- Jesus' eternal priesthood ensures His continual intercession for believers, highlighting His divine nature and everlasting role as high priest.

Perfect Sacrifice

Jesus offered Himself as the perfect and final sacrifice, surpassing the need for continual animal sacrifices.

1. Hebrews 9:12: "He did not enter by means of the blood of goats and calves; but he entered the Most Holy Place once for all by his own blood, thus obtaining eternal redemption."

- Jesus' sacrifice was once for all, providing eternal redemption and demonstrating the completeness and sufficiency of His divine act.

The Teachings of Jesus Christ

New Covenant Mediator

Jesus is the mediator of a new and better covenant, established on better promises.

1. Hebrews 8:6: "But in fact the ministry Jesus has received is as superior to theirs as the covenant of which he is mediator is superior to the old one, since the new covenant is established on better promises."

- The new covenant, mediated by Jesus, offers a more profound and enduring relationship with God, based on internal transformation and complete forgiveness.

Pioneer and Perfecter of Faith

Jesus is the pioneer and perfecter of faith, providing the ultimate example for believers to follow.

1. Hebrews 12:2: "Fixing our eyes on Jesus, the pioneer and perfecter of faith. For the joy set before him he

endured the cross, scorning its shame, and sat down at the right hand of the throne of God."

- Jesus' endurance of the cross and His exaltation serve as a model for believers to remain steadfast and faithful.

Living Out Faith

The practical exhortations in Hebrews guide believers in living out their faith through love, hospitality, purity, and contentment.

1. Hebrews 13:1-2: "Keep on loving one another as brothers and sisters. Do not forget to show hospitality to strangers, for by so doing some people have shown hospitality to angels without knowing it."

- These teachings emphasize the importance of practical expressions of faith, fostering a supportive and loving Christian community.

Drawing Closer to Jesus

The comprehensive picture of Jesus presented in Hebrews encourages believers to deepen their faith and draw closer to Him. By understanding His divine nature and unique role, believers are better equipped to appreciate the magnitude of His sacrifice and the depth of His love.

1. Hebrews 4:14-16: "Therefore, since we have a great high priest who has ascended into heaven, Jesus the Son of God, let us hold firmly to the faith we profess. For we do not

have a high priest who is unable to feel sympathy for our weaknesses, but we have one who has been tempted in every way, just as we are—yet he did not sin. Let us then approach God's throne of grace with confidence, so that we may receive mercy and find grace to help us in our time of need."

- Jesus' empathetic and accessible nature as the high priest invites believers to approach Him with confidence and find mercy and grace.

The book of Hebrews richly illuminates the divinity and teachings of Jesus Christ, providing believers with profound insights into His eternal and unchanging nature. As the high priest, perfect sacrifice, and mediator of a new covenant, Jesus stands supreme and unparalleled. By studying these teachings, believers are called to live out their faith with renewed confidence, perseverance, and devotion, anchored in the unchanging and ever-present Christ.

Through this exploration, Dr. Maxwell Shimba's work in "The Divinity and Teachings of Jesus Christ: Insights from the Book of Hebrews" has aimed to deepen the reader's understanding of Jesus' unique role and inspire a closer walk with Him. Embracing the truths of Hebrews leads to a more profound appreciation of Jesus' sacrifice, His ongoing intercession, and His ultimate authority, encouraging believers to hold firmly to their faith and live out the transformative power of the new covenant in their daily lives.